"I've battled against some of those profiled and heard some amazing stories about many of the others, so I am honoured to be included in *Hard Men of Rugby*."   – BAKKIES BOTHA
FORMER SOUTH AFRICA PLAYER & WORLD CUP WINNER

"It was safer and certainly more fun to read about the *Hard Men of Rugby* than to play against them! It's like having a few laughs over beers with them in the bar post-match, rather than what would have taken place on the pitch!"   – AL CHARRON
FORMER CANADA CAPTAIN & WORLD RUGBY HALL OF FAME INDUCTEE

"I couldn't put the book down. It was great to learn more about some of the hardest men in rugby folklore. And I had the misfortune to play against some of these legends!"
– BERNARD JACKMAN
FORMER IRELAND & LEINSTER PLAYER, COACH & COMMENTATOR

"A cracking read, with some great stories about some guys I played with and against. Plus many more I am relieved I never had to face."   – LEE BYRNE
FORMER WALES & LIONS PLAYER AND PUNDIT

"I laughed, winced and even found myself moved by this lively and fun rundown of rugby hardmen."   – BEN MERCER
FORMER RUGBY PLAYER & AUTHOR OF BEST-SELLING
FRINGES: LIFE ON THE EDGE OF PROFESSIONAL RUGBY

"Luke has uncovered some fantastic stories about some of rugby's most renowned characters, and in doing so has brought them vividly to life."   – ROSS HARRIES
BROADCAST JOURNALIST & AUTHOR

"Fresh, entertaining, well-researched and full of really fun nuggets."   – ROBBIE OWEN / SQUIDGE
YOUTUBER, PODCASTER & WRITER

HARD MEN of Rugby

Luke Upton

For Eimear, Iseult and Séamus.

First impression: 2020

© Copyright Luke Upton and Y Lolfa Cyf., 2020

The contents of this book are subject to copyright, and may
not be reproduced by any means, mechanical or electronic,
without the prior, written consent of the publishers.

The publishers wish to acknowledge the support of
The Books Council of Wales

Cover photograph: Getty Images
Cover design: Sion Ilar

ISBN: 978 1 912631 28 5

Published and printed in Wales
on paper from well-maintained forests by
Y Lolfa Cyf., Talybont, Ceredigion SY24 5HE
website www.ylolfa.com
e-mail ylolfa@ylolfa.com
tel +44 1970 832 304
fax 832 782

CONTENTS

"I told him if he wanted to fight, we could arrange that and if he wanted to play rugby, we would accommodate him there as well."

FOREWORD

by Nigel Owens

ONE OF THE questions I am regularly asked is whether I think the game has gone soft.

I always answer the same – absolutely not! The game is cleaner than it was, but that does not make it soft.

Some see the rugby of the 1970s or the 1980s as 'the good old days', but were those days really that good if the anecdotes about the dark deeds, the players getting booted at the bottom of the rucks, punches, stamps and headbutts were all true? Call me old-fashioned, but that's not the kind of game I would want to be part of and just because that stuff has been rooted out does not mean rugby is soft.

The pace of the game has picked up dramatically since I first picked up my whistle and so has the intensity and the time the ball is in play for. The hits today are thunderous, put in by blokes who are built like tanks. Yet I regularly see people picking themselves up off the floor and resuming play after being smashed square-on. The impact of collisions can be tremendous and the courage shown in every game never ceases to amaze.

Another popular question put to me is, who is the hardest player I've come across on the pitch? Well, many of the players included in this book would be very high up on my list, but when it comes to the hardest of all, I'm sorry Luke, it's not one of your selections! Though I can see one of your interviewees has agreed with me... it's Richie McCaw.

Capped 148 times by New Zealand, despite playing in the most attritional of positions, where every game he would be throwing himself into harm's way, perhaps by locking himself over possession and soaking up the attention of immensely powerful forwards who would do everything they could to wipe him off the ball. Now that's what I call a genuine hard man!

For me there's a huge difference between the hard player and the dirty player.

A dirty player is one that, for example, might deck someone with a cowardly punch from behind – something which in no way proves their hardness. In years gone by, before cameras and the citing commissioner, they might have got away with it had the officials missed it.

But not any more. With the advent of professionalism came sponsors' money and greater television exposure. TV shone a light on the thuggish minority, and the unions and clubs were aware that violent scenes would discourage parents from letting youngsters play the game and deter sponsors from wanting their name associated with such scenes.

So the game cleaned up, and my view is that today the sport is infinitely better. Rugby isn't as dirty as it once was, and this is something we should celebrate. There is more than enough scope to be hard and physical within the rules.

It's a privilege to be asked by Luke to write the foreword to this lively and engaging book. It's a great selection of players, some of whom I know personally. Others were far less familiar and it was fun getting to know them a little better. I hope you enjoy reading it as much as I have. For me, the big characters in rugby are what makes our sport so special, and there are some wonderful ones in here... even if they might have kept me very busy on the pitch!

Happy reading.

Nigel Owens MBE
Pontyberem, Wales, September 2020

INTRODUCTION

"I CAN'T BELIEVE you've not got him in there. C'mon, he's a right hard nut and he's won the World Cup and everything!"

This was the response from one of my mates on looking at my selection of profiles in this book. You too might have a similar view – your favourite rugby hard man might not be featured. Sorry: this is no criticism of the player (or you). The players profiled in this book are not meant to form an exhaustive or definitive list. I would expect many of the names to be familiar to you but others might be a surprise.

These hard men are instead a snapshot of 20 players across the eras of rugby union, from David Bedell-Sivright, the brooding Scot who caused havoc on and off the pitch in the years preceding World War I, through to the Argentinian firebrand Tomás Lavanini, who might have another ten years of playing ahead of him, if he doesn't get fed up with receiving lengthy bans for his frequent misdemeanours.

Nor is the list presented in order of hardness. In fact, there is no real order to how they are featured. Though there is one man who I think deserves the title of hardest of the hard men.

I have often been asked while writing this book, what is your definition of a rugby hard man?

There's a quote from Barry John which, although written in 1978, is still a good guide today: "It would be stupid, naïve and unrealistic to assume that in a game such as rugby with its physical side, everyone on the field would conduct themselves like perfect gentlemen, and play like chessmen. Players and referees alike accept the frustration that pure accidents can trigger off incidents where a fist or two will fly. The important factor is that these are not premeditated and are recognised as such or the referee has every right to act and give marching orders in such cases."[1]

I agree with Barry on the issue of premeditation being a defining aspect of being tough versus being dirty. So, with this in mind, there are two interlocked aspects in considering the players that have made my selection.

First, they are tough, uncompromising and physical. Perhaps they unflinchingly put their body on the line for their team, are fearless in tackling, brave under the high ball, seem immune to injury or are skilled in the dark arts of retribution, avenging some wrong (real or imagined) inflicted on a teammate. There will be a mental strength in there too: the overcoming of challenges and setbacks on and off the pitch.

Second – and just as important – they are very good players.

Put these two together, and the result is a player you want on your team and one who can be included in this selection. The criteria I have set rule out mindless thugs, cheats or cowards, and those super-tough guys who just weren't quite up to scratch at the top level of the game.

So, look at the list, think of your country or club in the era in which each individual played and consider if you would have had them in your team. I think the answer would be overwhelmingly 'Yes' in every case.

This book covers hard men of 12 different rugby nationalities, playing over a period of more than 110 years. Being an International rugby player in 1910 versus in 2020 would be an almost completely incomparable experience, and this impacts what a hard man today looks like. With sharper refereeing, television match officials (TMO) and post-match citings at the top level of rugby, it is harder than ever to get away with any misdemeanour.

But on the other hand, a huge tackle or feat of physical strength can go viral on social media, or become a hit on YouTube, instantly creating a hard-man reputation. One of our players selected has, as I make clear, had his career and bank balance benefit hugely from this kind of very modern reputation-building.

The shift from amateur to professional rugby in the mid-1990s is the great divide in this book. I don't think players are necessarily less tough in the modern era, but they don't have the hinterland that the amateurs do. The word 'amateur' has its origins in the Latin *amator*, meaning 'lover'; and from the perspective of today's game, there certainly seems something romantic about players doing regular jobs from Monday to Friday and then turning out in front of huge crowds at the weekends. But as discussed later, particularly in the chapter on Bobby Windsor, a love of rugby wasn't always that helpful in providing for a family.

Several of our amateur-era hard men were police officers, farmers, sailors or soldiers, and it is impossible not to factor this into how we judge their overall reputation.

Three of our selection, Robert Blair 'Paddy' Mayne, David Bedell-Sivright and Weary Dunlop, all saw active service in either World War I or World War II. And one did not return home. This too plays a role in their inclusion.

For some of the selection, their off-the-field activities or reputation factors into their inclusion, but their on-the-pitch ability still shines through.

Comparing the amateur and professional eras also makes a difference when it comes to the physical nature of players. Today's professionals are bigger, faster and stronger than their amateur-era counterparts. To give one example, Colin 'Pinetree' Meads, was 6' 4" tall and tipped the scales at 15st 7lbs, and was considered a giant of the game in the 1960s. Today, he'd still be big, but Irish centre Robbie Henshaw or All Black winger Julian Savea are the same size as him. Players who stand out because of their physicality are increasingly rare. If anything, particularly small players are noticed more now.

A final note is that I've also used a traditional definition of 'tough' in making my selection. A different definition might see me including the likes of Matthew 'Hambo' Hampson, the England U21 prop who became paralysed from the neck down after a scrummaging accident and has since dedicated his life to tireless charity work with his foundation. Or David Pocock, the Australian flanker who has been vocal on a number of issues including climate change and same-sex marriage, and was arrested in 2014 after locking himself to digging equipment for ten hours, protesting against the expansion of a coal mine.

It would certainly include those players and administrators who put pressure on apartheid-era South Africa and faced vehement opposition, sometimes even from their own teammates. And, no doubt, the female players fighting for more opportunities to play the game would also be there, plus the first wave of gay and lesbian players and officials who went public with who they love.

These rugby players and many, many more have all risked far more than a black eye or red card for their actions.

All things considered, in making this selection I wanted tough guys, good players and great stories. The world of rugby is a fantastic one: it is varied, passionate, sometimes inconsistent and maddening; but despite all its changes, its players remain its beating heart. Some are bad, some might be a little bit mad, but all make it the game we love.

Of all the quotes about the players I've included in this book, there is one that stands out for me on the role a hard man can play. It comes from Glenn Ennis, on his late Canada teammate Norm Hadley: "Real toughness on the rugby field is measured in how you could affect those around you. Norm always made us more confident, and our opponents less so."

I believe this is true of all the men in this book and I hope it does justice to them and the world in which they played.

PADDY MAYNE

"Mayne was a Viking, a throwback to the
ancient days of towering warriors."

FACTFILE

Full name: Robert Blair 'Paddy' Mayne

Born: 11 January 1915, Newtownards, County Down,
present-day Northern Ireland

Died: 14 December 1955, Newtownards, County
Down, Northern Ireland

Position: Lock

Representative teams: Ireland, British & Irish Lions

Clubs: Ards RFC, Malone RFC

Nickname: the Phantom Major

SLEEP WAS HARD to come by on the Lions tour of South Africa
in 1938.

At 3 a.m., following an official dinner, George Cromey – a
talented fly half who, when not slotting kicks, was delivering
sermons in his role as a Presbyterian minister – had just nodded
off when he was awoken by a loud crash. He sat bolt upright.
The door had been flung open and a large shape stood in its
frame. Cromey blinked heavily, then squinted in the half-light
to see who had disturbed him. Slowly the man came into focus;
he was a wearing the dirtied remains of black-tie, including
a tattered cummerbund, but something large and misshapen
seemed to be draped across his shoulders.

"I've just shot a springbok," bellowed the voice.

Cromey wouldn't have been surprised as to who had woken him. The light flicked on and there was his fellow Ulsterman, Robert Blair 'Paddy' Mayne, upon whom Cromey had been foisted to be a calming influence. Rather than retire for brandy and cigars with his teammates, Mayne had sneaked out from the dinner to join a late-night hunting trip.

"Jimmy Unwin has been complaining that the meat here isn't as fresh as it is back home," Mayne said. Cromey's reaction has not been recorded, but one suspects if there wasn't too much mess, the good Reverend would have quietly sighed and sunk back under the covers.

Mayne now took himself off to Unwin's room, broke down the door and hurled the springbok onto his sleeping colleague. The English winger was fast asleep and understandably panicked at such a rude awakening, and scrambled to escape the bloody mass lying top of him. In the chaos, he cut his leg on the poor beast's horn.

Mayne wasn't quite done. He scooped the springbok up from the bed and headed to the nearby room of the South Africa manager, leaving it outside with a daintily handwritten note saying it was "A gift of fresh meat from the British Isles touring team".

Now, we all love rugby tour stories. From International tours to the smallest village team, everyone has one. His antics with the springbok alone would be enough to have Paddy Mayne inducted into the all-time High-jinks Hall of Fame. But for the robust lock forward, this barely makes the Top 20 of his escapades. And unlike the vast majority who pull on that famous Lions jersey, this peak of rugby representation was not to be the greatest honour bestowed upon him.

Robert Blair Mayne, mostly known during his playing career and since by his nickname 'Paddy' – a moniker that was in part born of ignorance as he was from the Protestant, Unionist tradition, and a name that he was not particularly fond of – was born in Newtownards, County Down, the sixth of seven children in a prominent local family. His talent for rugby was first spotted at Regent House Grammar School, and he played for the school first XV and his local club Ards RFC from the age of 16. A keen all-round sportsman, he took up boxing whilst studying law at Queen's University in Belfast and won the Irish Universities heavyweight title in August 1936.

At just 22, in 1937 he made his Ireland rugby debut in a 5-3 win over Wales at Ravenhill and the following year he was selected to become a Lions tourist. Whilst planning for Lions tours is now dominated by wrangling over schedules, club commitments and sponsor demands, tours of old had few such worries. This one lasted three months and took in 24 matches, including a two-match sojourn into Zimbabwe (then known as Rhodesia). While the Lions lost the Test series 2-1, their victory in the final game was the first Test win for the Lions in seven and their first win against South Africa since 1910.

Mayne played in all three Tests and 17 of the club matches, and despite the series defeat, his performances greatly enhanced his reputation. *The Northern Whig*, a Belfast-based newspaper, reported on his performance in that first Test, stating, "Mayne was outstanding in a pack which gamely and untiringly stood up to a tremendous task." In the third Test, which the Lions won, the same newspaper told its readers, "Mayne was outstanding in the open and magnificent in defence."[2]

Rob Cole, respected rugby journalist and author, supported this contemporary analysis of Mayne's performance. "Where he led, others followed on the field. He tackled and carried hard, never shirked his work at the set pieces and loved nothing better than when the game cut up rough. As a former Irish Universities heavyweight champion, he was more than able to hold his own when the action heated up."[3]

But hunting Springboks on and occasionally off the pitch only tells part of the story of Mayne's South African summer. This was a tour where lots of drink was taken and Mayne seemed to be always at the heart of it. Like rock bands of the 1970s, he had a habit of smashing up hotel rooms and kicking down doors when drunk. Although a quiet and focused individual when sober, with a fondness for the poetry of A E Housman, he loved company when he drank, and found it hard to find teammates who could keep pace with his demands.

But in William 'Bunner' Travers, the 25-year-old Newport and Wales hooker, he found something of a kindred spirit. Sharers of many beers in hotel bars and pubs throughout the tour, it was also reported they'd dress as sailors to get into scraps in the ports of Durban and East London. But it was in Johannesburg that their most infamous act took place.

Temporary stands were being erected for the Lions fixture at the city's rugby ground, Ellis Park, by a work gang of convicts, who slept in a compound beneath the scaffolding. Strolling around the ground ahead of the game, Mayne and Travers engaged one prisoner in conversation and were shocked to find he was serving a seven-year stretch for stealing chickens.

Determined to right what they saw as a major miscarriage of justice, they returned later that night armed with bolt cutters, a new set of clothing and a determination to help the man they'd nicknamed 'Rooster' and another prisoner escape. They duly set the men free, but their liberty wasn't to last long, as both were recaptured the following day. When Rooster was collared, the jacket he was wearing had Mayne's name stitched inside it.

Mayne can consider himself lucky he didn't find himself in custody. Following this incident, he was told to room with Reverend Cromey, but that did little to change his ways, as the springbok-hunting incident showed.

He had a good friend in his captain and fellow Ulsterman Sam Walker, who intervened on at least six – yes, six! – occasions on the tour to stop him being sent home early. It also helped that Mayne was as disciplined and focused on the pitch as he was freewheeling and wild off it.

The debt to his captain was repaid in part at least during one particularly physical tour match, where a cheap shot on Walker knocked him out. As he lay on the floor, slowly regaining consciousness, he looked up to see two stretcher-bearers running over to where his assailant was now lying motionless on the ground. Mayne strolled over and with a barely contained smile said, "Don't worry Sammy, it's sorted."[4]

Walker had his own views on his saviour that day, seeing him as "quiet, soft-spoken, self-effacing off the field, but in the heat of the match he could be frightening. He was the toughest and strongest man I have ever known. James Clinch, a tough man himself and one of the great Irish International players, once confided in me that the only man he ever feared on a rugby field was Mayne."[5]

Mayne may have only made one Lions tour, but his legacy lived on – as another Irish Lion, Mike Gibson, who toured in the 1960s and 1970s, explained. "In my early days with the Lions, Harry McKibbin, another member of that 1938 tour, spoke to us about the huge role Blair Mayne had. He made a real impact on the field on that tour. He was a colossus – physically strong and imposing, and back then there were not as many huge rugby players."[6]

Having returned from the Lions tour, there was still rugby to be played. More appearances for Ireland followed for Mayne, as did the high jinks. He threw an Irish teammate out of the window of a Swansea hotel during some post-match celebrations. Fortunately it was only a ground-floor window, so no major harm was caused.

But the fun and games of rugby would have to be put aside as World War II began. 90 Internationals were killed in the conflict, including one of Mayne's Lions and Ireland teammates and fellow Queens University graduate Robert Alexander, who lost his life fighting in Sicily in 1943, aged just 32.

For Mayne however, if he found a release in playing rugby, he found his true purpose in soldiering, in a wartime career that could have been peeled straight from the pages of a *Boy's Own* adventure – but one that perhaps never left its main character feeling satisfied.

Prior to the outbreak of World War II, Mayne joined the reserve. At the outbreak of hostilities he first received a commission in the 5th Anti-Aircraft Battery, then in April 1940 joined the Royal Ulster Rifles, and following Dunkirk, volunteered for the 11 (Scottish) Commando. As a second lieutenant, he first saw action in 1941, fighting fascist French forces in Syria and Lebanon, where he was awarded a mention in dispatches.

It was around this time that Mayne's reputation reached Lt. Col. David Stirling, commanding officer of the recently founded Special Air Service (SAS) – the elite British Special Forces unit. The romantic, though almost certainly untrue, story of them meeting has Mayne languishing in a Cairo jail for hitting his superior officer over mistreating his dog.

After outlining his invitation to join the nascent formation, the probably apocryphal tale has Stirling – himself a tough and complex character – telling an initially sceptical Mayne, "There's one more thing. This is one commanding officer you never hit and I want your promise on that." Mayne shook his hand, and a partnership even more fearsome than that with 'Bunner' Travers was forged.

From November 1941 to the end of 1942, Mayne took part in many night raids against Axis forces in the deserts of Libya and Egypt. He pioneered the use of jeeps for rapid, surprise attacks. Mayne's first major success was in leading a six-man team on a raid on Wadi Tamet airfield that destroyed 24 aircraft and a fuel depot on 8 December 1941. For this, he received his first Distinguished Service Order, and this action also dampened down calls from some traditional quarters of the British Army who wanted to disband a unit that prided itself on its unorthodox attitude and a relaxation of the stuffy norms of military rule and regulation.

Audaciously, he would return to the same airfield later that month to destroy a further 27 enemy planes. Even when his unit ran out of explosives, the damage continued, with Mayne reportedly ripping electrical equipment from cockpits and dashboards with his bare hands. These North African raids continued and by the end of the war, reports suggested that Mayne was responsible for the destruction of up to 150 aircraft.

David Stirling was captured in January 1943, and the 1st SAS Regiment was reorganised into two separate parts: the Special Raiding Squadron (SRS) and the water-based Special Boat Section (SBS). Mayne was given command of the SRS throughout 1943.

With the Axis powers driven out of North Africa, Mayne's next campaign was in Italy in 1943. Bringing his men ashore under fire at Augusta in Sicily, he led the charge from the landing craft and secured the beach, allowing a larger force to follow. For this Mayne received the first bar to his Distinguished Service Order. The official citation reads as follows:

> The landing was carried out in daylight – a most hazardous combined operation. By the audacity displayed, the Italians were forced from their positions and masses of stores and equipment were saved from enemy demolition. In both these operations it was Major Mayne's courage, determination and superb leadership which proved the key to success. He personally led his men from landing craft in the face of heavy machine-gun fire. By this action, he succeeded in forcing his way to ground where it was possible to form up and sum up the enemy's defences.[7]

The following year, always in the thick of the action, he was parachuted behind enemy lines in the Battle of Normandy to conduct reconnaissance before resuming his use of jeeps for fast, deadly attacks on Germans, carrying out many raids throughout the second half of 1944. For these he was awarded the second bar to his DSO. Whilst fighting in France, he worked closely with the Resistance, and the post-war French government awarded him both the *Légion d'honneur* and the *Croix de Guerre* – the first foreigner to receive both.

By 10 April 1945, the war was coming to an end, but the fighting remained ferocious. Near the town of Oldenburg in Germany, an SAS unit was ambushed and pinned down and their commanding officer killed. Mayne received a message from the stranded troops, jumped into a jeep and drove straight into the action. Against overwhelming odds, he systematically killed or forced most of the Germans into retreat, but several of his wounded SAS comrades were still pinned down under heavy fire in a ditch. I'll let the official citation tell you what happened next:

> Any attempt at rescuing these men under these conditions appeared virtually suicidal owing to the highly concentrated and accurate fire of the Germans. Though he fully realised the risk he was taking, Colonel Mayne turned his jeep round once again and returned to try and rescue these wounded. Then by superlative determination and by displaying gallantry of the very highest degree and in the face of intense enemy machine-gun fire, he lifted the wounded one by one into the jeep, turned round and drove back...[8]

For this feat of daring, he was recommended for the Victoria Cross (the highest and most prestigious award that can be given to UK military personnel), but was instead awarded a third bar to his DSO.

Why did he not receive the Victoria Cross? Well, throughout World War II he retained his hard-drinking, abrasive ways, regularly clashing with those in authority over him. Plus, many in the regular army viewed the role of special forces with some suspicion (the SAS was actually disbanded for a few years after World War II ended) and so didn't wish to see further praise heaped upon its leaders. Perhaps being Northern Irish didn't help either?

David Stirling said it was a "monstrous injustice" that Mayne didn't receive a VC, adding, "it was the faceless men who didn't want Mayne and the SAS to be given the distinction."[9]

Sixty years later, in 2005, there were still calls for Mayne to receive a VC, with more than 100 MPs supporting a motion that stated:

> David Stirling, founder of the SAS, has confirmed that there was considerable prejudice towards Mayne and that King George VI enquired why the Victoria Cross had 'so strangely eluded him'... therefore calls upon the Government to mark these anniversaries by instructing the appropriate authorities to act without delay to reinstate the Victoria Cross given for exceptional personal courage and leadership of the highest order and to acknowledge that Mayne's actions on that day saved the lives of many men and greatly helped the allied advance on Berlin.[10]

A Victoria Cross can be awarded posthumously, but the motion was defeated and it still eludes Mayne. The question is: would he have cared? I suspect not.

There's a parallel world where a 35-year-old Mayne goes on the Lions tour to New Zealand, Australia and Ceylon in 1950, perhaps not playing in the Tests but still leading from the front in the midweek club games and enjoying the post-game socials. An elder statesman giving advice to the younger tourists on the dark arts of the scrum and, if the mood and perhaps the drink so took him, regaling them with some of his war stories.

But it is not the real world.

With the war over, Mayne had a spell with the British Antarctic Survey in the Falkland Islands, but his time in the South Atlantic was cut short by a crippling back complaint that had begun during his army days. He returned home to Newtownards and a law practice. His back problems worsened, not only stopping him playing rugby, but even standing on the terrace to watch it as a spectator. Like so many ex-service personnel, the return to provincial humdrum life proved as challenging as his time in uniform. Posthumous psychological assessment is not possible and might appear presumptuous, but with what we now know about Post Traumatic Stress Disorder (PTSD), what causes it and what the symptoms look like, there are indications that Mayne may well have been suffering from it.

In the excellent *Rogue Warrior of the SAS*, which details Mayne's life, the authors neatly sum up these post-war years: "People who knew him in his latter days could be divided into two categories: those who were proud to be in his company, and those who were afraid to be. For there were two Blair Maynes. On one hand, the gentle giant, soft-spoken, self-effacing, unfailingly considerate and polite; on the other hand, the touchy, quarrelsome and dangerous human animal which emerged when – as we say in Ireland – drink had been taken."[11]

On 13 December 1955, following a Masonic meeting, he was drinking and playing poker at a friend's house. He decided to drive home in his Riley sports car at 4 a.m., but never made it. Just a few hundred yards from his home, he struck a parked lorry and crashed into an electrical pylon, dying instantly.

He was 40 years old.

Mayne's home town came to a standstill, and his death was mourned not just in Northern Ireland but by a vast and varied number of former teammates and opponents as well as brothers in arms across the world.

Mayne never married nor had children, but decades after his death, his name still lives on in both sporting and military circles, and his influence on SAS tactics prevails to this day. A forthcoming BBC One drama about the early days of the SAS is planned, with Tom Hardy reportedly in line to play Mayne, and this will no doubt further reignite interest in the Ulsterman.

When you look beyond the reputation, the headlines and the medals and a life is truly examined, it can be complex. He was far more than the rugged war hero Lion that a sketch of his life might portray.

In 2011, Mayne's secret World War II diary was found and excerpts published. In addition to casting further light on the battles in which he fought, the diary also helps paint a picture of the real Mayne and his relationship with his mentor Stirling.

Military historian Gordon Stephens explained to the BBC, "Mayne had to come back from an operation and he didn't like that. When Stirling got back from the operation, Mayne had gone into a tent and started drinking. Everyone expected a big punch-up between these two great warriors of the SAS.

"Stirling tells the story that he went into the tent and Mayne was there reading James Joyce and he looked up and said, 'All I wanted to do was write,' and Stirling sat down with him, poured another whiskey and said, 'All I ever wanted to do was paint.'

"These two great SAS figures sat down and discussed painting and writing. That's the other side of Mayne people don't know about," concluded Stephens.[12]

We'll probably never know the true Mayne. But we do know he was a fantastic rugby player and an even better soldier.

I'll leave the last word on him to the late Seán Diffley, the grand old man of Irish sports writing, who wrote of him, "Mayne was a Viking, a throwback to the ancient days of towering warriors, gentle and charming when in repose, but fierce and dangerous when aroused, and a 'hyphenated' nuisance when he had a couple of jars."[13]

BRIAN LIMA

"They said that every time I connected a tackle, they could hear bones clicking!"

FACTFILE

Full name: Brian Pala Lima

Born: 25 January 1972, Apia, Samoa

Positions: Wing, Centre

Representative teams: Samoa, Pacific Islanders

Clubs: Marist St Joseph's, Ponsonby, Auckland, Blues, Highlanders, Stade Français, Swansea, Secom Rugguts, Munster, Bristol

Nickname: the Chiropractor

RUGBY NICKNAMES ARE a rich, humorous and sometimes mildly obscene part of the game. From the ubiquitous 'big' or adding 'ers' to the end of the surname, at the other end of the scale you have the more ingenious examples, such as English centre Billy Twelvetrees being called '36' after one of his Irish clubmates pointed out that in his accent 'twelve trees' total that number. Australian legend John Eales, a goal-kicking, twice World Cup-winning lock, was called 'Nobody' because "Nobody's perfect". Another favourite is former Wales winger Chris Czekaj, who was nicknamed '28' by his teammates at Cardiff. Why? Well that's how many points you would get in Scrabble for his surname!

In the amateur era, the professions of the players – in law, agriculture or the police – often led to their on-field nicknames.

But Brian 'the Chiropractor' Lima has no formal medical qualifications. What he does have is one of the most fearsome reputations of any player in the professional era.

If you were looking for an Exhibit A to support this reputation, you would point to a moment in the 2003 World Cup when Brian Lima's Samoa were facing off against South Africa. The game was over as a contest, with the Springboks 34-10 to the good and on the attack. The late, great Joost van der Westhuizen spun a high pass out to his half back partner, the 20-year-old Derick Hougaard, impressing in just his fourth cap. The young outside half paused for just a second to glance right to see what was available, and then boom, lights out.

He'd been hit by Lima, who came hurtling out of his defensive line straight into Hougaard, knocking the Springbok hard into the turf, the ball popping up into the air like a champagne cork. It was very hard, but legal. Hougaard lay spread out on the floor, play continuing to his right.

He'd just met 'the Chiropractor'.

This tackle perfectly illustrates Lima's physicality and ferociousness, even when the result was all but decided. But this match was remarkable in another way: it came 16 years after his World Cup debut.

In his first World Cup, the 1991 edition, the 19 year old became the then youngest player to take part in the tournament, and was part of the Western Samoa team that beat Wales 16-13 in Cardiff. The Samoan physicality was a shock to the undercooked Welsh team, leading Ieuan Evans, the Welsh captain, to admit to the press post-match that each contact saw his boys "knocked back a couple of yards at a time".

The late, great Frank Keating, reporting for *The Guardian*, wrote the following day, "In its long history the Arms Park cannot have witnessed such a sustained and devastating display of tackling. Time and again ball-carrying Welshmen at full pelt were clobbered amidships and thundered back a yard or more... Some sixth sense must have inspired the Welsh management, weeks ago, to book the whole squad into the Penoyre Rehabilitation Centre for Sports Injuries near Brecon today. Some will be booking in for bed and several breakfasts, poor Wales. By the end, even smugly smiling Englishmen in the crowd were wincing for the Welsh."[14]

It was the start of Lima's career, but only partly into Wales' deep decline. As the final whistle went, the quip went round Cardiff Arms Park, "Thank heavens Wales weren't playing the whole of Samoa!"

Speaking to me from his home, Lima says that day remains a big moment, not just for him personally but for the country as a whole. "This remains one of my best memories of my rugby career. We were hurting because we didn't make the inaugural Rugby World Cup in 1987 so were determined to make our mark, and boy, did we do that! We relished our underdog status. No one knew who we were. In fact it felt like no one even knew where Samoa was! We were pretty much written off. The players had boundless self-belief and big hearts and when no one else expected us to beat Wales, we believed we could and it was the best feeling ever when we did. That was the game that put Samoa on the map!"

Brian Pala Lima was born in Apia, the capital of Samoa, and gave *The Daily Telegraph* a little insight into how his early years influenced his style of play. "We used sticks for balls, because we had nothing else. It made it very difficult for opponents to get them off you. As a boy in Samoa, I was always playing rugby. It was natural to play anywhere there was some spare ground. Everyone liked to see who could put in the biggest and hardest tackle. Everyone challenged each other."[15]

Lima played for Ponsonby and then, after rugby union went professional, had spells at New Zealand Super Rugby outfits the Otago Highlanders and the Auckland Blues (with whom he won the title) before heading to the northern hemisphere.

During this period, he gained his famous nickname. Lima tells us more: "I got it in 1996, which was my first Super 12 year with the Otago Highlanders. John Leslie, the captain of the Highlanders at the time, and the other boys started calling me 'the Chiropractor' so I asked John why. He told me that a chiropractor is a doctor who can click bones, literally. They said that every time I connected a tackle, they could hear bones clicking! Hence the nickname! I'm not sure I liked it at first but after all these years, I don't mind being called it."

Leaving Super Rugby, he joined crack French outfit Stade Français (where he won the Top 14), then a pre-regional rugby Swansea, where he combined with fellow hard man Scott Gibbs (profiled later in the book). Next he moved to Munster (though injury stopped him ever making an appearance), then Japanese side Secom Rugguts. He finished his career with Bristol in the English Premiership, retiring from club rugby in 2007. Opponents in the six leagues he graced must have drawn a sign of relief when they heard the news.

Remarkably, despite a glittering club career, it is probably his appearances at five World Cups – the only player to have achieved this feat – for which he is best known. After his debut in 1991, he reached the quarter-finals of the 1995 tournament, losing to eventual winners South Africa; four years later he returned to defeat Wales in Cardiff again, though a play-off defeat to Scotland denied Samoa a second successive quarter-final. In 2003, despite spirited performances, and giving poor Hougaard quite the jolt, Samoa went out at the group stage.

I asked Lima to share with us what he remembers of this famous tackle.

"South Africa are always one of the best teams in the world and they were hot favourites against us. As always, we went out there to play and give it our all, but we also knew we needed a lot of physicality to match the South Africans. I remember this particular play well. I played in the midfield and, fortunately (but maybe unfortunately for Derick!), once we were penalised, it was easy to read the play. As soon as Joost quick-tapped the ball, I could see our fly half Tanner Vili had him, and knew he had to pass to Derick. So with the benefit of time, I saw the perfect opportunity to line him up and nail a good tackle.

"It's always a good feeling to have the timing right and make the tackle as near to what you plan as possible. As soon as I connected, I knew I had nailed it, and my immediate thought was to look to see where the ball had gone. The adrenalin is something else. As you know, Samoans love to tackle and tackle hard. It's all in the timing and it's all about attitude. This for me ranks as one of my most memorable tackles," added Lima with a chuckle.

From the receiving end of this mega-hit, this is what Hougaard recollected when I spoke to him: "The Brian Lima tackle! To be honest, I'd not seen him before that day in Brisbane. But, oh my word, did I feel him! Joost took a quick tap and threw a high pass out to me. My first thought was to catch the ball above my head as soon as possible, open up my body and quickly spread the ball wide. But Brian had other ideas! Bang! Immediately I thought I had broken something."

Hougaard continued, "Luckily the play went on for many phases and I spent some time in the foetal position trying to catch my breath. The team doctor said they must replace me. But although I was struggling to speak, I told him that I was just winded and was slowly able to stand up. Once back on my feet, I walked over to Joost. Remember, I was only 20 years old. I told him, 'Please keep the passes a little bit lower.' And immediately he was angry at me! I said, 'You must be kidding. I almost got decapitated. And you are angry at me!'

"Years later, when Joost got sick, I spent a lot of time visiting him, and spoke about the game and his experiences. One day when I went to see him, he said, 'I have a present for you,' and pulled out a Brian Lima jersey! He finally apologised for that pass and we both had a big laugh. I'll treasure that shirt forever.

"I managed to continue playing and got some respect from my teammates and the fans. But I still get asked about that tackle. I always reply the same – my jersey was wet but where he hit me was completely dry! I took the hit. And it was a great one. It was Samoan rugby at its best. I respect the man and he put us together in history forever. One day me and Brian will have a cold beer together!"

In Lima's final World Cup, 16 years after his first, Samoa again failed to escape from the pool. After their last game of the tournament, a win over the USA, he led several celebratory performances of the Siva Tau (Samoan haka) before being carried around the pitch on his teammates' shoulders to generous applause from the crowd.

Lima himself hadn't actually featured in that fixture, however. Why not?

He was serving a three-week suspension after being cited for a tackle on England's Jonny Wilkinson the previous week. Whilst the referee awarded only a penalty, the citing commissioner saw it as a stiffer offence and, on review, World Cup judicial officer Professor Lorne Crerar agreed. Crerar said the tackle was "inherently dangerous", and Lima's swinging right arm had connected with "considerable force" to Wilkinson's neck and throat area. A three-week suspension heralded the end of his World Cup and his International career.

After retirement, Lima and his family moved back to Samoa and since then he has continued his involvement in rugby through coaching. He has acquired a Level 3 coaching qualification which has enabled him to be involved at the national level, through coaching Samoa A and also having a spell as assistant coach for the national sevens team, as well as extensive grassroots coaching at his local club, Marist. On top of coaching, he also runs sessions and bootcamps at local gyms. Lima tells me his commitments as a family man keep him busy the other half of his time.

He's deeply proud of Samoan culture and I asked him why physicality is such a part of their rugby. "I guess it is because of the way we have been brought up in our families. From a young age, the boys do most of the physical work in the families, villages and their communities. Therefore, when it comes to sports, they bring a lot of that physicality into the game."

This is something that the countless players who have had an unscheduled appointment with 'the Chiropractor' will testify to!

WAYNE SHELFORD

"I told him if he wanted to fight, we could arrange that and if he wanted to play rugby, we would accommodate him there as well."

FACTFILE

Full name: Wayne Thomas Shelford

Born: 13 December 1957, Rotorua, New Zealand

Position: No. 8

Representative teams: New Zealand Māori, New Zealand

Clubs: Auckland, North Harbour, NZ Combined Services, Northampton, Rugby Roma

Nickname: Buck

WHEN NEW ZEALAND lifted their second World Cup in 2011, their inspirational captain Richie McCaw was hiding a secret as he hoisted the trophy aloft. The back row had actually played the bulk of the tournament with a broken foot. He had first injured it in preseason training in January 2011, suffering a stress fracture that required the insertion of a pin. It was aggravated in the group match win against France, but through adrenaline, willpower and some serious painkillers, he made it through three more games to lift the Cup and end a 24-year drought for the rugby superpower.

"He can hardly walk and how he played today, I just don't know," All Blacks coach Graham Henry told journalists after the game.[16] Post World Cup, X-rays revealed that he hadn't just aggravated the original injury but also suffered a second fracture. The postscript to this is perhaps even more remarkable: McCaw would recover from these injuries, play another four years and lift the World Cup again in 2015.

McCaw's battle against injury pales into insignificance, however, when compared to what fellow Kiwi World Cup-winner Wayne 'Buck' Shelford overcame in 1986, during the infamous 'Battle of Nantes' International against France. He had made his New Zealand debut the week before in a 19-7 win over the same opponents in Toulouse, but this second Test would be a different story. The home team were ferocious in their ambition to avenge the previous week's defeat. Early on, Shelford took a kick to the face, and had four teeth knocked out. He played on.

Then, on 20 minutes, he was holding on to the ball at the bottom of a ruck, when a stray (or intentional?) *Les Bleus* stud connected with his groin, where it tore his scrotum, leaving one testicle hanging out.

"It bloody well hurt," said Shelford, unsurprisingly. "I chucked some of the proverbial Jesus water down my shorts to make it feel better. That didn't do a lot so we just played on."[17] And play on he did.

It was only when, at another ruck a few minutes later, a Frenchman came flying in from the side and knocked Shelford unconscious that he had to be helped gingerly from the pitch.

But this was not the end of the game for Shelford. As the Kiwi physio examined him, he noticed the scrotum injury, and decided to stitch it up. On the touchline. To add to this moment of black humour, the French TV producers decided to turn the cameras onto this scene and viewers were treated to footage of some particularly delicate stitching of his most sensitive area, beamed straight into their living rooms.

The already surprised French must have been gobsmacked when, his patch-up complete, Shelford trotted back onto the pitch to recommence playing. It was only deep into the second half that a further blow to the head left him unable to complete the match.

"I was knocked out cold, lost four teeth and had a few [actually 18] stitches down below," recalled Shelford, speaking years later to the BBC. "It's a game I still can't remember – I have no memory of it whatsoever. I had to watch a video to realise what the game was actually like. I don't even remember what the score was. I don't really want to either."[18]

For the record, New Zealand lost 16-3. It was the only time Shelford was on the losing side during his distinguished International career.

In his official biography, Shelford described this defeat as a "mental and physical disaster... it became a distressing setback to me and the team's Test record."[19]

The 'Battle of Nantes' was already an infamous chapter in the history of International rugby, but then in 2015 the French team doctor of the 1980s, Jacques Mombet, was interviewed by French investigative journalist Pierre Ballester for his book *Rugby à Charges: L'Enquête Choc* (The Case Against Rugby: The Shock Investigation).

What he said proved explosive and made public for the first time the rampant drug-taking by French rugby players during this period.

"Amphetamines have always existed in rugby and elsewhere," Mombet told Ballester. "In the 1970s, entire teams were taking them... I remember a Championship match – between Fleurance and Marmande, I believe – in which the referee was scared! The players were all foaming at the mouth. He had to stop the game."

Mombet said the drug-taking was most obvious when France played New Zealand at Nantes in 1986. "They each had their little pill in front of their plates for the meal before the match. The All Blacks realised that their opponents, unrecognisable from the previous week, were loaded."[20] He stated that the New

Zealand management made a complaint to the International Rugby Board post-match, which did eventually lead to a clampdown on drug use.

Shelford himself was not surprised when the book detailing the drug culture in French rugby during this period came out, as he recalled the pre-match moments.

"When I came out of the tunnel and I saw them, I looked into the eyes of many of the players as I walked past them, and their eyes did not say that they were going into a game against the All Blacks," he told Radio New Zealand in 2015. "Their eyes just looked like they were on something, and I could not prove it."[21]

Perhaps despite having four teeth knocked out, having his scrotum torn, and being rendered unconscious, Shelford was actually lucky to escape without worse punishment that day.

The defeat in Nantes looms large in Shelford's career, but should not overshadow his fantastic playing ability, or the other times when he proved his hard-man credentials.

Born in 1957 into a large, rugby-mad family in Rotorua, Wayne Thomas Shelford acquired his nickname 'Buck' due to having very prominent teeth in secondary school. Aged 17, he joined the New Zealand Navy, where he juggled playing rugby and travelling around the Pacific on various postings.

He played for Navy teams and various club outfits before joining the newly formed North Harbour in Auckland, and becoming their first All Black.

In 1987, a year after the 'Battle of Nantes', the inaugural World Cup was held jointly in Shelford's native New Zealand and Australia, and it provided the opportunity for a rematch with the French. The All Blacks' passage through the tournament was largely trouble-free, but controversy would engulf Shelford in their semi-final match against Wales. And testicles would once again be involved.

Welsh lock Huw Richards had been tussling with New Zealand's Gary Whetton, and according to Shelford had "grabbed him by the testicles and was given a solid elbow for his troubles". Taking exception to this, Richards hit the Kiwi lock with a right-left combination that put him on the floor. All hell broke loose. Shelford blindsided Richards with a huge right hook that knocked him straight out. Wales prop Anthony Buchanan responded with a punch straight to Shelford's jaw. But the Kiwi did not go down.

Worse was to come for a dazed Richards: once Welsh physio Tudor Jones had brought him back to consciousness and he had uneasily stood up, he was rewarded with a red card. Whetton and Shelford both avoided any further punishment. And 14-man Wales went on to lose 49-6. Richards was the first man ever to be sent off at a World Cup, with the tally even after the card-heavy 2019 tournament still at only 24. Whilst he continued to enjoy a good club career with Neath, he never played for his country again.

Speaking to *The Daily Telegraph* in 2011, Richards stated, "I don't regret what happened. It was one of those things that goes on in rugby. I just happened to be the one who copped the punishment. I took a few elbows, but that seemed to go under the radar. The officials missed that. They saw me as the aggressor and decided to send me off.

"I played the game hard and saw no problem in sorting things out on the pitch. It was part and parcel of the game. So, you can imagine how frustrated I was when I saw the ref pointing to the touchline. It wasn't far to go, but it felt like a very long walk," concluded Richards, who had long held a silence about that day. He is now kept busy by a large sheep farm on the slopes of the Brecon Beacons.[22]

Shelford has a slightly different view of proceedings, writing in 1990, "I saw what was happening and thought 'enough's enough', and belted Richards. I connected fairly well and, as he went down, I was hit from the side [the Buchanan punch] and had a tooth broken... Paul Moriarty [a Wales forward, with his own reputation for fiery behaviour] was circling about looking to carry the action on. I told him if he wanted to fight, we could arrange that and if he wanted to play rugby, we would accommodate him there as well.

"By then referee Kerry Fitzgerald was sorting out the trouble... after Richards came to, he was ordered off. I guess that was fair because he had begun the fracas, while Fitzgerald said he couldn't officiate on my actions because he hadn't seen my punch. I got a bad name out of the situation, wrongly I believe, but it has made the opposition wary of me."[23]

Speaking in 2019 to Wales Online, Paul Moriarty recalls of Shelford, "He was actually a decent bloke, a hard man – obviously – but I didn't find him dirty. Back then it was a different sport and there were more flare-ups."[24]

Nowadays, there would likely have been a citing of Shelford and a suspension from the final, but no such punishments existed in 1987. He therefore took his place in the New Zealand side that managed to gain revenge for the defeat in Nantes with a 29-9 win over the French in the final, and lifted the first ever World Cup.

Following this triumph, Shelford assumed the captaincy of New Zealand and under his leadership between 1987 and 1990, the All Blacks did not lose a single game. In 1989 they won all 14 of their games on a tour of the UK and Ireland, scoring 454 points and conceding a mere 122.

Shelford's replacement in the New Zealand team in 1990 by Zinzan Brooke proved controversial, and led to public outrage and a national campaign to 'Bring back Buck'. He never played another Test, but signs with this phrase urging the All Black management to reinstate him would appear for years to come. And not just at rugby matches, but also at cricket, soccer and even the Olympics – and now they have drifted into meme culture. The spectre of Shelford would haunt his replacement Brooke, who – whilst fantastically talented, with his flashier style of play and occasional penchant for kicking the ball – proved quite the opposite to Shelford, and never fully convinced swathes of the All Black faithful that he should be wearing the No. 8 jersey.

In 22 Test matches for his country, that loss to France in Nantes was the only time Shelford tasted defeat.

In 1991, he received an MBE for his services to rugby and moved to England to play for Northampton for three years, revitalising the team and instilling his own high standards at the Midlands outfit. He retired from playing in 1995 after a spell playing in Italy at Rugby Roma, and took up coaching positions at Saracens and Rugby Lions in the UK and North Harbour and North Shore in his native New Zealand.

It would be remiss to write a profile of Shelford without mentioning his involvement in the Cavaliers, an unofficial New Zealand team that toured apartheid South Africa in 1986. An official 1985 tour was cancelled following intense political pressure and legal action that successfully argued it would contravene the New Zealand Rugby Union's constitutional promise to promote, foster and develop the game.

But with some private backers, sponsorship from the South African *Yellow Pages* and a desire to prove themselves as the best team in the world, the vast majority of the New Zealand squad jetted off to South Africa and into a whole heap of controversy. The only absentees were scrum half David Kirk and a then 19-year-old John Kirwan, who objected to the tour on moral grounds.

Although they won seven of their eight club games, the Cavaliers lost three of the four Tests. Few sports team had toured apartheid South Africa, and the tour was globally condemned and deeply controversial in New Zealand itself – probably more so than the players had expected.

On their return, the NZRFU barred the participants for two games, their places filled by the 'Baby Blacks' who went on to form the basis of the most successful period of All Blacks rugby. Although Shelford would be welcomed back into the fold, other Cavaliers struggled to get their places back.

In his 1990 book, Shelford issued a passionate defence of his actions, seeing politics as something that shouldn't be involved in sport. "We felt justified in going to the Republic because we objected to being dictated to by the politicians in New Zealand... Our democratic rights had been usurped the year before and we were determined it wouldn't happen again."[25]

He added, "We didn't travel to South Africa to alter the political scene. We talked and met people and played our rugby – that was our way of trying to break down barriers." He concluded, "It was a great tour and even now I look back and say it was the greatest tour of all."[26]

Despite the controversy around this Cavaliers tour, he still stands alongside fellow hard man Colin 'Pinetree' Meads in the pantheon of legends in the eyes of most New Zealand rugby fans; yes, because of his tough, uncompromising, skilful play, but also because of the importance he put on Māori culture within rugby.

The haka – an ancient posture dance of the Māori, traditionally used to prepare a war party for battle – has been performed pre-match by the New Zealand national team since the early part of the twentieth century. Its fearsome delivery is now known globally even by those who aren't rugby fans. But it wasn't always performed with the same zeal or commitment. A quick search on YouTube for 'Old School Funny Haka' illustrates this perfectly in the performance by the team ahead of a game v. Barbarians in Cardiff in 1973. It's less a war dance, more a lost Monty Python sketch.

It was Shelford, himself of Māori descent, and teammate and Rotorua school friend Hika Reid who changed what the haka meant to New Zealand, and turned it from a bit of a jig with little cultural impact into something powerful. The change began following a discussion with the team about whether they should even do the haka on a tour to Argentina in 1985. Shelford and Reid stated that that it should be only done if everyone was fully behind it and understood truly what it meant. The team put it to the vote and agreed – with just one dissenting voice – to learn the correct words and actions.

So they set to work. The two men led training sessions as they would with any other new rugby skill, not just focusing on the moves and the *whakahua* (pronunciation) of the dance itself but also talking about wider Māori culture, laws, traditions and customs. Soon players from Māori and *Pākehā* (non-Māori) heritages bought into performing the haka with the precision and intensity that we are now accustomed to.

Before the 2019 World Cup, Shelford spoke to *Rugby World* about how he changed perceptions of it. "Those sessions were bloody hilarious. Big, proud, butch men being asked to shed their inhibitions and do a dance – some of them just had no rhythm whatsoever and had to learn how to just hang loose. By the '87 World Cup it was a different prospect altogether."

It's hard now to imagine the New Zealand rugby team without the haka, and today it is without a doubt the most recognisable symbol of Māori culture and probably of New Zealand itself.

"I'm proud," continued Shelford, "of the way it's grown and my role in that. It shows off Māori culture. Māoridom has filtered more prominently into other aspects of Kiwi life since the haka's revival – every school has one [its own haka], there are tourist attractions, Māori art is more popular and companies' logos are embossed with Māori designs in a way that they weren't years ago."[27]

In 2007 Shelford faced a battle with his hardest opponent yet – Non-Hodgkin Lymphoma, a cancer that attacks the lymph nodes while weakening the immune system. After six months of intensive chemotherapy, Shelford made a full recovery but was warned of the high chances that his cancer would return, and has since been a prostate cancer ambassador.

Today Shelford is often called upon as a spokesman for men's health issues in New Zealand. He has a particular focus on young men getting themselves checked and taking better care of their health and wellbeing, both physical and mental. When Kiwi flanker Liam Squire made himself unavailable for the 2019 World Cup, citing mental health problems following a series of injuries, Shelford quickly and publicly spoke out in support of the decision.

Wayne 'Buck' Shelford had a remarkable career, being in the final wave of players who successfully straddled a career outside rugby (in the Royal New Zealand Navy) with playing rugby at the very highest level. His hard-man credentials are unchallenged – his sickening injury and Lazarus-like recovery at the 'Battle of Nantes' see to that. Never losing a Test as All Blacks captain and playing in a World Cup-winning team would be enough for legend status. But the part he played in revitalising the haka into the brutally majestic performance we see today, and his current focus on the health and wellbeing of young New Zealanders confirms his place in the very elite of world rugby.

BOBBY WINDSOR

"We had to beat bigger packs by skulduggery and there were times when we played like a gang of thugs."

FACTFILE

Full name: Robert William Windsor
Born: 31 January 1946, Newport, Wales
Positions: Hooker, Loose-head prop, Tight-head prop
Representative teams: Wales, British & Irish Lions
Clubs: Whiteheads RFC, Newport Saracens, Cross Keys, Cardiff, Pontypool, Pontypool Athletic
Nickname: the Iron Duke

EVEN FOR THE illustrious Wales team of the 1970s, a trip to France proved daunting. The likes of Gareth Edwards, J P R Williams and Gerald Davies and their fellow rugby immortals won five Five Nations Championship titles, five Triple Crowns and three Grand Slams in this golden decade. They had an 80%+ success rate against England, Ireland and Scotland during this time. But this dominance didn't extend to fixtures against *Les Bleus*, and certainly not in Paris, where they suffered losses in 1973, 1977 and 1979.

So the selection of six new caps for the opening game of the 1975 Championship at the Parc des Princes was a bold – perhaps some would say foolhardy – move. The half-dozen were flanker Trefor Evans of Swansea; Steve Fenwick, who would mark his debut with a try alongside the ebulliently complex Ray Gravell in the centre pairing; Aberavon's John Bevan, who slotted in at outside half; and two props, Charlie Faulkner and Graham Price, both of Pontypool.

Remarkably, all six would go on to play for the Lions, and the 25-10 victory on their Wales debut would vindicate the brave selection and pave the way to winning another Championship. The day was capped by a remarkable try by Graham Price, who, after kicking the ball down field, galloped 75 yards before picking up the loose ball with some neat handiwork to dive over in the corner. Not bad for a prop! "They'll never believe it in Pontypool," were Nigel Starmer-Smith's words on the BBC commentary as Price sprang up from the muddy pitch, arms aloft and just a little bit out of puff.

Few that day would have imagined that Wales would have to wait 24 years for their next win in the French capital, a run that included 11 consecutive defeats for the men in red.

But the woes could wait – this was the peak of the champagne era of Welsh rugby. This five-try rout was their biggest win in Paris since 1909. And if this day wasn't special enough, packing down between Faulkner and Price was their Pontypool teammate Bobby Windsor, making this Wales' first ever one-club front row.

The legacy of that day loomed large in the Welsh psyche for decades to come thanks to singer-songwriter Max Boyce, who penned 'The Pontypool Front Row' on his number one album, *We All Had Doctors' Papers!* as a tribute to Messrs Faulkner, Windsor and Price.

> There's a programme on the telly, I watch it when I can.
> The story of an astronaut, the first bionic man,
> He cost six million dollars,
> That's a lot of bread, I know
> But Wigan offered more than that
> For the Pontypool front row![28]

That song also christened the front-row combination the 'Viet Gwent', as a nod to the Viet Cong, the Vietnamese and Cambodian military that had recently defeated the USA in the Vietnam War. Now, Graham Price, with his blond curls and taciturn manner, and Charlie Faulkner, more outgoing and with a certain mystery about his date of birth – estimates for his age on his debut varied between 27 and 30 – would both be worthy of inclusion in this book, but it is the third in the triumvirate, Bobby Windsor, who just edges it.

In his excellent autobiography, *The Iron Duke – The Life and Times of a Working-Class Rugby Hero*, he neatly summarises his approach to hooking in the 1970s:

> We had to go in and punch and boot like mad. Sometimes, against bigger sets of forwards, the only way we could beat them was by pure violence. We'd do things the other home countries wouldn't do. We'd rip into them, intent on causing injury... You stamp on someone's head, he goes off, has some stitches and comes back. Stamp on his ankle, he doesn't come back. A lot of the players who did things like that wouldn't dream of admitting to it, but that was how the game was. The darker parts, like the scrum, could be very nasty and you had to be nasty to survive.[29]

Windsor was born in 1946, among the first wave of baby-boomers, his father having just returned from war service with the Royal Navy. The Newport into which he was born was dominated by industry and in particular steel, and it was the steelworks where he worked for most of his career and where he began playing his rugby. His first club was Whitehead RFC, originally founded as a works team for the Whitehead Iron and Steel company, and he rose through the club levels before joining Pontypool in 1973. The club was a founder member of the Welsh Rugby Union, and it was under a decade of captaincy from Terry Cobner in the 1970s that 'Pooler' became one of the all-time great club teams of Welsh rugby. No one was more important than Windsor in securing this reputation.

A legendary scrummaging front row, he was heavier, at 16+ stone, than most hookers at the time. Windsor tended to hook with his head before driving – there being no law at that time about keeping your shoulders above the hips as there is now. And typically, when it was the opposition's put-in, he wouldn't bother with the opposition's hooker, instead focusing on their tight head. His knowledge of the front row was such that he actually played for Pontypool as a loose-head prop, and even appeared for the Lions as a tight head. In the loose he was mobile, a strong runner with a very low centre of gravity. When Windsor got going with the ball, he was tough to stop.

The past, as they say, is another country, and never is this more apparent than when looking at the life and career of Bobby Windsor. Whilst without a doubt he had the skills to prosper in the current day – his mobility is certainly a trait of the modern hooker – his life and approach to the game were firmly rooted in industrial south Wales.

Firstly, there was the work: leaving school at 15, he worked in various jobs, including in a cake factory and as part of the concrete gang working 12–14 hours a day building the M4. He also had a spell, perhaps unsurprisingly, as a nightclub bouncer, but it was the steelworks where he earnt a crust for most of his career. Hard and physically demanding shift work, it also delivered a financial challenge. Pay at the steelworks was largely based on the amount of steel produced a week. So if you weren't working, you'd only receive a meagre basic wage. Amateurism was zealously enforced in those days and so for Windsor, who married young and quickly became a father to a growing family, the cost of representing first Wales and then the Lions had to constantly be weighed against making ends meet domestically.

He was always looking to earn a few extra pounds, and wasn't opposed to making the most of any opportunity that came his way. Arriving at the training camp for his first Lions tour, he found himself unsupervised in the kit room.

"It was all lovely gear, loads and loads of it. I went round once and no one seemed to notice, so I went around again. And again. Whatever I didn't need, I shoved into bags... As a thank you to my mate, I gave him some stuff so he could sell it when he got back to Wales and give the missus money to help her pay the bills while I was away. Nobody was any the wiser. I found out later that there were more people wearing Lions gear in Pontypool than in the whole of South Africa!"[30]

These were long tours as well, not the slimmed-down versions we see now – they averaged three and a half months in the 1970s. Windsor wasn't the only one to have to navigate the financial challenges of being an in-demand rugby player. To take a snapshot of his fellow Lions tourists in 1974, Ian McGeechan had to suspend mortgage payments whilst he was away from his teaching job and Andy Irvine never got another day's holiday from his employer after using so much going to South Africa.

Secondly, there was a level of brutality in 1970s rugby that has long retreated under the glare of television, post-match citings and professionalism. It was the 1974 Lions tour to South Africa that cemented Windsor's reputation, taking his brand of abrasiveness beyond just south Wales and the Five Nations and into rugby's most brutal heartland.

The scene was set at a pre-departure team meeting in a London hotel, when the inspirational and granite-hard captain Willie John McBride gave one of his rousing speeches: "If there's anyone here with any doubts, go home now. Not a word would be said... I've been in South Africa before and there's going to be a lot of intimidation, a lot of cheating. So if you're not up for the fight, there's the door."

There was a brief silence as the team contemplated the challenge, then Windsor jumped up and shouted, "I'm going to bloody love this!"[31]

Shortly afterwards, Windsor further outlined his perspective on the prospect of the 1974 tour, as remembered by fellow tourist, Scottish winger Billy Steele. "We were asked if we had anything to say. 'Yeah, I do,' he said. 'When I'm down on the deck and these bastards start kicking me and stamping on my head, I don't want to look up and see the numbers on your back. I want you right there with me.' Talk about a key moment. That was the tour on the road."[32]

Those managing this Lions tour had, as players, lost in South Africa before, and placed the blame on a lack of fight, in every sense of the word. So in response, McBride instigated the famed '99 call' – originally called 999, but they quickly realised on this tour that even milliseconds count. It was brutal in its simplicity and simple in its brutality. If a Lion was in trouble and the call went up, each of the tourists would get stuck into a Springbok, irrespective of what they were doing or of the guilt of their opponent. The logic was to show the Lions would not be intimidated, with a second theory that if every single player was involved, then the referee couldn't send everyone off. The call was used several times during the tour – most famously in the third Test, when the Springboks were desperate, having lost the first two Tests. As all hell broke loose, infamously J P R Williams ran half the length of the pitch to land a punch on the huge second row Johannes 'Moaner' van Heerden.

The results of the tactic were not always pretty but they worked. The Lions won 21 of their 22 matches, with only a dubious draw in the final fixture saving the home nation from a 4-0 Test whitewash. The Lions crossed for 107 tries and conceded just 13.

The Springboks' reputation as the hard men of world rugby had taken a battering, and Windsor, who played in each of the four Tests, had been instrumental in their pulverisation. He recalls the second Test in particular. "We went into that first scrum and squashed them. I had a good feeling from then on. Their front row was screaming for help. When you're down there and you've got the upper hand, the best sound in the world is to hear that 'awwwww!' from the other lot because it tells you they can't take the hit. They were gasping a lot in the Tests and it was music to our ears."[33]

Returning triumphant to Wales from South Africa, it was back to work at the steelworks and in the Five Nations. More Championship wins and Grand Slams were to come, but it was his battles with his French opponents that became legendary.

Windsor recalls one International match where Alain Estève kicked him in the face and at half-time he planned his revenge. "I bided my time, knowing I'd get my chance. When it came and he was on the ground, I booted him in the mush as hard as I could and that started a fight. At least I thought that we'd seen the back of Estève. How wrong can you be? Once the ref had calmed down, I saw Estève get to his feet and walk back. Then he turned round in my direction and gave me a wink. And I thought 'Oh, f**k me. There's going to be hell to pay any minute now.'"[34]

The game continued to be a fiery affair. But after the match, Estève took Windsor on a tour of Parisian nightclubs, of which he had extensive knowledge, going "from being my worst enemy to my best friend, all in the same day and night".

Such was the respect they had for him across the Channel that it was a president of the French Rugby Union who, at one post-match dinner, christened Windsor the 'Iron Duke' – a nickname first given to Arthur Wellesley, the Duke of Wellington; another man who knew a few things about defeating the French under difficult conditions.

Windsor would be selected again for the Lions in 1977, although this tour to New Zealand would ultimately end in disappointment. The tourists had their chances of glory, but succumbed to a 3-1 Test series defeat. The success for Wales continued, but his final International, in 1979, was a defeat to his old nemesis France. The club games, though, would keep coming: his last appearance for Pontypool, who were one of Wales' most dominant teams for large stretches of his career, was not till 1987 – the 556th senior game he played.

It would be easy to cast Bobby Windsor as something of a stereotype, tending the steel mills in the week, then applying brute force and no little skulduggery at 2.30 on a Saturday afternoon before some noisy pints in the clubhouse. But dig a little deeper and you see a far more complex character.

He suffered terrible tragedy in 1979, when his wife Judi, mother of his three young children, died of cancer aged just 33. He would later remarry and have three further children, but in 2006, after he himself was diagnosed with prostate cancer and had suffered domestic and business difficulties, he sat on a cliff top in west Wales with a box of paracetamol, intending to commit suicide. Fortunately, one of his sons found a note he had left, had a hunch as to where he would go and found him just in time. Windsor battled back from this period of depression and now lives in sunny retirement, playing golf and fishing in Puerto Portals, Mallorca, though he regularly returns to Wales and can often be found opining on the modern game.

And yes, he does think it's gone soft.

What do Sam Warburton and Bobby Windsor have in common? Are both Welsh rugby legends? Yes. Huge figures on successful Lions tours? Yes. Did they both display total commitment to winning? Yes. Aside from that, I think you might be struggling to find more similarities. There's Warburton, the career athlete whose reward for a win over England might be an extra piece of chocolate, and Windsor, the steelworker with no need for a gym, whose clubhouse pints were part of his post-match warm-down.

But they have one other aspect in common, both having received one red card in their career. Warburton, as you'll no doubt remember, got his in the World Cup semi-final versus France in 2011, while Windsor's was shown for knocking out a Swansea player whilst turning out for Cross Keys in 1972. All the battles, all the scrapes, all the punches and kicks (given as well as received), and he had the same number of early baths as the squeaky-clean former Wales captain.

Eddie Butler, broadcaster, journalist and teammate at Pontypool, is clear in his reverence for the hooker from Newport. "Bobby Windsor was the best player I ever played with. Simple as that. He was also vicious; the most cold-hearted brute you would never wish to see standing over you at a ruck... He was also sublimely skilful, a good footballer who was very quick, especially off the mark... Some hookers are good at some parts of their trade and not so good at others. Bobby was the master of all of them."[35]

Windsor cuts a remarkable figure in Welsh rugby, embodying both something special, and something that has been lost. He is unique to that particular era of Welsh rugby, the alliance of bankers and brickies, farmers and pharmacists, doctors and dockers who took the sport to new heights.

Yes, he was hard, very hard, and he definitely crossed the line – to be honest, the line was sometimes a bit of a blur – but you can't be so consistently successful for club, country or the Lions without being a superb player. When it came to the jungle warfare of the front row, no one could defeat the Viet Gwent, and even today their legend looms large over those who crouch, touch, pause and engage every weekend.

COLIN MEADS

"For one with Meads' worldwide
reputation for robust play, this [red card]
was rather like sending a burglar
to prison for a parking offence."

FACTFILE

Full name: Sir Colin Earl Meads KNZM, MBE

Born: 3 June 1936, Cambridge, Waikato, New Zealand

Died: 20 August 2017, Te Kuiti, Waikato, New Zealand

Position: Lock

Representative team: New Zealand

Club: King Country

Nickname: Pinetree

THE INSTRUCTIONS FOR the East Transvaal team against the visiting New Zealand side in 1970 were simple, and they came from the very top. The president of the South African Rugby Board, Danie Craven, publicly stated a hope the provincial teams would "soften up" the tourists, but there was nothing squidgy about the attitude they brought into this fixture.

On six minutes, with New Zealand already a converted try to the good, Colin Meads, who at 34 had lost none of his appetite for the game, was lying on the ground at a ruck when a boot came flying in, aimed firmly at him. With no chance to avoid or lessen the blow, it powered into his arm, causing a clean break in his radius, the outer of the two bones in his forearm.

Meads' Kiwi teammate Earle Kirton, speaking in 2016, has vivid recollections of that game. "There were boots flying everywhere at the bottom of the rucks. I can remember him [Meads] saying to me, 'Shit, it's like duck-shooting season down here. They're all over the bloody place.'

"They were going to make sure that the Test players got roughed up a bit... I went down on the ball and he [Meads] said 'I'm coming up.' Then I heard a whack. Someone had booted his arm where he had his arms around me on the ground, covering me up. I said, 'Oh sugar. I mean, heavens. Aw shit, Pinetree, you haven't broken it, have ya?'"[36]

Broken it he had, but he played on.

After 20 minutes and barely able to use his arm, he went over to the sideline to talk to the doctor. "It was tingling and the doctor that examined it said he couldn't tell what was wrong. And then he said he didn't think it was broken. I thought, 'I'm not going off if it's not broken, I'd be a wimp if I went off just because somebody had kicked my arm.'"[37]

In the 1970s, replacements were allowed, but only after a doctor had verified the player could no longer continue. So Meads returned to the fray, playing 76 minutes of a brutal game with a broken left arm. The visitors ran out 24-3 winners. After the match, the All Blacks' changing room resembled a field hospital, with 12 players suffering injuries, including torn ankle ligaments and several broken noses among the 'softening up' they'd been given.

When an X-ray later confirmed the break, Meads famously muttered, "At least we won the bloody game."

This would not be the end of the story, or even the end of Meads' tour.

Yes, he missed the next couple of games and the first Test, but he got a bespoke arm guard made in Cape Town, and with permission from referees and the South African Rugby Board, extraordinarily he was back playing by the middle of the tour, and started both the last two Test matches.

Colin Meads was not merely the most famous All Black of his era, but is one of the most famous New Zealanders of all time. His prowess and longevity make him the equivalent of Australia's Don Bradman at cricket, or Babe Ruth in American baseball. In 1999 he was named New Zealand Player of the Century and the International Rugby Hall of Fame, on welcoming him, described him as "the most famous forward in world rugby throughout the 1960s".

Born in Cambridge, in Waikato on the upper North Island of New Zealand, in 1936, he grew up on the family sheep farm near Te Kuiti, where he spent all his adult life. Family lore states that his great-grandfather Zachariah Meads left his home in Wellington at the age of just 12 after an argument with his father, and walked 120 miles to where the Meads family farm would flourish. The mix of uncompromising rugby and the farming life characterised a rugged masculinity that has long been central to many New Zealanders' sense of self. Although even during his International career – a remarkable 133 games (55 of them Tests, then a record) for the All Blacks between 1957 and 1971 – this view, and the country itself, began to change.

After making his senior rugby debut in 1955 aged 19, Meads played his entire provincial career – 139 matches – for King Country. These formative years proved influential in how he'd play the game. He recalled in 2002 that inter-provincial rugby back then was full of "hard bushmen who played to win and knocked the hell out of each other in the process. There were some skilful backs but generally it was a pretty bruising, brutal sort of game up front, and that was the way it should be, as far as they were concerned."[38]

Within two years, he'd been capped fully for his country, initially as a flanker and No. 8, and he remained a near-permanent fixture in the team for 14 years.

The nickname 'Pinetree' was given to him by teammates on a New Zealand U23 tour of Japan, and its immediate origins don't relate to his size, as you might assume. Meads himself recalls it being more to do with him looking like someone else a few of his teammates had known with the same moniker. At 6' 4" tall and tipping the scales at 15st 7lbs, he was big but no giant, and would certainly be on the smaller side for a lock today. But the nickname stuck, and through his career he was also known by variations of it: 'Piney', 'Tree' or even 'the Tree'.

"I don't mind what they call me," said Meads, "and anyway there wasn't a lot I could do about it. I answer to any of them now. I've been called worse!"[39]

His son Glynn, a talented player who would himself turn out for King Country for a decade, finishing up as captain, naturally was given the nickname of 'Pinecone'.

When people talk about Meads, there's a normally a mention of the physicality, perhaps his mythical training with a sheep under each arm, probably playing on with a broken arm against East Transvaal, but also perhaps how his actions ended the career of Ken Catchpole, the Australian captain and scrum half, during a Test match at the Sydney Cricket Ground in 1968.

"That incident," said Meads, "was one of things that tarred me. Of course, I felt sorry for Catchy, but I never felt guilty about it."[40]

The Australian team of the later 1960s did not have too many players of international renown, but they did have Ken Catchpole. A super-quick scrum half with an accurate pass and a keen sense for gaps and opportunities, he became the Wallabies' captain just shy of his 22nd birthday. As a result, he was one of the few Australian players the New Zealanders marked out as a threat, and he was treated accordingly.

During the first half, Catchpole was moving from the typical position of the scrum half and coming into spaces usually occupied by the forwards, and burrowing deep into rucks to get the ball. The word from an unimpressed All Black coach Fred Allen came through: "For Christ's sake, put the little bastard on the ground, then see if he wants to keep coming back in amongst you, you big soft so-and-sos."

Just after half-time, Catchpole was caught.

Buried at the bottom of a ruck, the ball in his hands but unable to move, one of Catchpole's legs was protruding through the tangle of bodies. Meads saw an opportunity. He grabbed the leg and yanked it with all his might. The other leg couldn't move. If you can picture a wishbone, the oddly shaped forked bone found in poultry, then that will give you an indication of the anatomy here. Catchpole was defenceless, and had his "muscles stretched like rubber bands until they snapped".[41]

The Australian captain's hamstring was torn from the pelvic muscle, severely damaging his groin muscles and sciatic nerve. He was stretchered off the pitch in agony and would never play rugby again.

Meads maintains that he didn't know the other leg was pinned as he pulled him, and he did attend a testimonial dinner for Catchpole, who never (publicly, at least) held a grudge.

The rugby community of Australia did, however. Former Wallaby forward Keith Cross was so incensed at the incident that he sent Meads a newspaper cutting graphically describing Catchpole's injuries. With it he included a note that read, "Colin, are you proud of this effort?"

"The referee did not penalise me, but in the eyes of the Australians, I was just a dirty big bastard," Meads wrote shortly afterwards. "All Australians thought I was a blood criminal and I know Australia has still got this against me."[42]

The referee that day, Roger Vanderfield, was a doctor and would have been in little doubt as to the seriousness of the injury, but no action was taken against Meads. He played on and New Zealand won 27-11.

A year earlier at Murrayfield it had been a different story for Meads.

During this period, the northern and southern hemispheres had different interpretations of killing the ball. Europeans thought it perfectly fine for a player to simply lie on it until backup arrived. The rest of the world, and in particular New Zealand, viewed this as obstruction and, as such, deemed it perfectly legitimate to ruck the man off the ball, with either feet or hands. This was a major point of contention during inter-hemisphere matches, and it was this interpretation that was to see Meads receive the kind of punishment he evaded the following year in Sydney.

Just three minutes from the end of the match, New Zealand were winning 14-3 when the Scotland outside half David Chisholm landed on a loose ball and was promptly kicked hard by a chasing Meads. Yes, he did get some of the ball, but much more of the Melrose man. The Kiwi skipper, sporting a complex-looking head bandage (on account of a tussle with some French forwards the previous week) which added to his intimidating appearance, had already been warned once by Irish referee Kevin Kelleher for dangerous play. And with this second serious offence, he was asked to leave the field.

The crowd went wild as the Kiwi talisman trudged off the pitch. His reputation ensured he was already something of a bogeyman to European rugby fans as it was, but even more of a shock to the watching Scots was that players back then simply didn't receive sanctions like this. There were no touch judges, no TMO and no post-match citings. So if the referee missed it (or chose not to see it), then no action would be taken.

It was 42 years since the previous International player had been sent off – another New Zealander, Cyril Brownlie, at Twickenham in 1925 for stamping on an England player lying face down on the pitch. Remarkably, the next All Black to receive a red card after Meads was Sonny Bill Williams, who received his marching orders 50 years later in the second Test against the British & Irish Lions, for a dangerous shoulder-charge on Anthony Watson. What this says about New Zealanders being saints on the pitch, or having an undue influence on referees, is not for this book to judge!

The Daily Telegraph drily noted on the red card, "For one with Meads' worldwide reputation for robust play, this was rather like sending a burglar to prison for a parking offence."

Fred Allen saw things differently, however. "I think crowd hysteria influenced the referee, Irishman Kevin Kelleher. Colin's head was all bandaged up as a result of the injury he'd got in Paris, so he looked a bit scary. But I'll swear on my deathbed that he didn't intend to kick the half back, Chisholm. I was just so sad seeing that big guy I liked and respected so much trudging off the field. Quite wrong."[43]

Meads disagrees with Kelleher's verdict as well. "I always considered myself a fair player. Even though I was sent off for allegedly kicking Chisholm at Murrayfield, I didn't and wasn't kicking at him. I kicked at the ball. I admit I retaliated at times, and that didn't help my image. It got me into a bit of strife."[44]

Nonetheless, Meads was worried that the red card would spell the end of his career. Nothing could have been further from the truth. He returned home to a hero's welcome and would soon be exchanging Christmas cards with Kelleher. His career in the All Black shirt would continue until 1971, ending with the classic series defeat to arguably the greatest ever Lions team.

If truth be told, other red cards could have easily come his way. He broke the jaw of Wales hooker Jeff Young with a punch during a tour match in 1969. Though Young would admit he was being a nuisance throughout the game, and was known for his own rambunctious style, his teammates saw things differently. Flanker Dai Morris remembers the match well. "It was my first encounter against the All Blacks in a Welsh jersey, a team I much admired. I had less admiration for them when the great Colin Meads broke Jeff Young's jaw. There was some jersey pulling, but the reaction was ruthless and unwarranted."[45]

John Dawes, the Welsh centre, was also unhappy at what he saw that day. "We were very bitter and it would be silly to say we were not. Young pulled a front row forward's jersey. But instead of the New Zealander concerned doing something about it, Meads threw a punch and broke his jaw. Meads had nothing to do with the incident... It wasn't Meads' fight and we were bitter he hit Jeff Young when he was unprepared."[46]

Meads both gave and received some serious punishment on the pitch, but he didn't see himself as a dirty player. "There were a lot of players at the top level who would kick the proverbial out of you. I never condoned that, and I never did it. I saw it as cowardice. And I copped a fair bit of it."[47] He had no problem with his opponents playing as hard as him, and enjoyed his battles with the likes of Ireland's Willie John McBride and Benoît Dauga of France, forming lifelong friendships with many of his adversaries.

Meads had something of an ogreish reputation to many, and yes, there were dark moments in his career, but his ability as a player should never be overlooked. He wasn't merely an enforcer. The leading light in a legendary forward pack, alongside players such as his brother Stan and other Kiwi greats Wilson Whineray, Brian Lochore and Waka Nathan, he was part of a New Zealand team that enjoyed huge success during this period. His handling and passing was slicker than nearly any other forward of the time, and his play in the loose would regularly contribute to tries – he notched up 28 in the 133 games he played for the All Blacks.

Upon retiring, whilst continuing to farm, he moved into coaching and administration and was the All Blacks' team manager at the 1995 Rugby World Cup. Later he would become a renowned after-dinner speaker, normally appearing with a beer in one hand, drily recalling tales of the good old days of amateur rugby. However, he always noted that these past times, with their tours lasting several months, put severe financial pressure on the family farm.

Colin Meads died of pancreatic cancer in 2017 at the age of 81, and was survived by Verna, his wife of 60 years, 5 children, 14 grandchildren and 7 great-grandchildren. Meads' casket was protected by Māori warriors who then performed a haka at his *marae* (memorial service). Across New Zealand, people placed rugby balls outside the front door of their homes in a show of respect to the man many saw as epitomising not just New Zealand rugby in the twentieth century, but the country as a whole.

Speaking on Meads' death, New Zealand Prime Minister Bill English recalled a lot of fond memories, and stated his belief that Meads "represented a lot of what people think it means to be a Kiwi". This son of the soil, with his physical, no-nonsense approach to rugby and life, but always happy to have a beer and enjoy a joke when the work was done, resonated hugely in a period when New Zealand, still a relatively young nation and still dominated by agriculture, was seeing its rugby team become its most famous export.

A hard man, without a shadow of a doubt, but Meads' time as an All Black had a far bigger influence than just his actions on the pitch.

There's one postscript to the Meads story that will be of particular interest to England rugby fans. Martin Johnson (profiled later in the book), at just 19 and after impressing in a junior tournament, was approached by Meads to come to New Zealand and play for his King Country side. Meads took a special interest in this raw English lock, perhaps seeing something of himself in his glowering, unrelenting approach to the game. But after watching his underwhelming first two games, he gave him some advice: "Martin, you've got to get more aggressive. You are allowed to hurt the opposition when you've got the ball. People don't realise that. You're a big unit. When you get the ball, you're in charge of the whole game. You're allowed to knock some bugger over. You've got to get more aggressive."[48]

Johnson listened and went on to play two successful seasons, appeared in a black jersey for the New Zealand U21 side and even met his future wife in the area before returning home. Johnson credits the physicality of playing rural rugby so far from home, under the watchful eye of Meads, with giving his career a major early boost. So England perhaps in a small way have Pinetree to thank for their 2003 World Cup triumph, for having shaped one of its lead architects.

JERRY COLLINS

"If you were carrying the ball, you always felt he was hunting you down, that he was coming."

Full name: Jerry Collins
Born: 4 November 1980, Apia, Western Samoa
Died: 5 June 2015, Hérault, France
Position: Flanker
Representative team: New Zealand
Clubs: Wellington, Hurricanes, Toulon, Ospreys, Yamaha Júbilo, Narbonne
Nicknames: JC, the Terminator, Cement

DEFINITION OF A ringer: A person highly proficient at a skill or sport who is brought in to supplement a team.

In amateur sports, they are typically a mate or a cousin who is drafted into the team at the last minute. They normally play for someone else or have extensive experience and tend to raise the standard of the team. In schools' rugby they would sometimes be accused of being older than they actually were – the lad with the beard playing U14s, for example.

What they are typically not is a 26-year-old All Black, whose last game had been a World Cup quarter-final. And certainly not when appearing for South West 2 West division club Barnstaple RFC, who play in the fifth tier of English rugby. But then there was nothing typical about Jerry Collins, and the story of how he turned out in a Devonshire grudge match against Newton Abbot is just one of many that made the man so special.

So how did he end up in Devon in the autumn of 2007?

Rewind a few weeks and Collins had been in the starting XV for New Zealand when they were knocked out of the World Cup in a shock defeat to France in Cardiff. It was the latest in a run of surprise World Cup defeats for the All Blacks dating back to 1991 and the response back home was a mix of incredulity and anger. To take time out of the glare, Collins went down to Croyde in Devon for some surfing and much-needed rest and recuperation.

He was spotted in a café by the Barnstaple head coach, Kevin Squire, who went over to have a chat and invite him down to the club. He didn't think too much more of it, so imagine his surprise when Collins pulled up at the ground. He spent the evening with the team and even coached a session for the U14s.

As the evening wound down, Squire cheekily asked if he fancied a game. "I told him we had a match coming up and he was welcome to join us, but again I was gobsmacked when he showed up to catch the bus with the rest of the players."[49]

The league's rules forbade him from registering for the first team, but the regulations around the second XV were more relaxed, so whilst still on the books of Wellington-based Super Rugby outfit Hurricanes, he was on for his Barnstaple RFC debut against Devon rivals Newton Abbot.

"It was very surreal for the lads as they are all amateurs – most are builders, bricklayers, plumbers and so on," said Mr Squire. "He had even been to a sports store to buy a new pair of boots."[50]

Whilst getting changed pre-match, Collins called his New Zealand colleague Dan Carter, beginning the call by exclaiming, "You wouldn't believe where I am!" What Carter replied wasn't recorded, but he likely didn't say 'north Devon'.

Collins played barely at half speed but still managed to score a try and made three try-saving tackles, most notably when he scooped up an opposition winger who thought he was leaping through the air to score a try and carried him back down the pitch. Unsurprisingly Barnstaple won 21-7.

He'd retire from Barnstaple with a 100%-win record, but the story wouldn't quite end there. Back in the clubhouse post-match, Collins asked his Barnstaple teammates if he could wear their club socks while playing for the Barbarians against South Africa at Twickenham a month later.

"There is Jerry Collins of New Zealand and Barnstaple," said commentator Stuart Barnes as the All Black smashed into one of his shuddering, trademark challenges in front of 58,000 fans, wearing his red and white Barnstaple socks.

His Devonshire cameo neatly summed up Jerry Collins: he was a hard-man enforcer dominating the back row, but was also full of generosity and was a rare colourful figure in the professional era. He played in some of the top leagues and biggest games, collecting 48 Test caps for New Zealand and captaining them three times, but for him rugby was always meant to be fun.

Collins was, like fellow hard man Brian Lima, born in Apia, Samoa, though he moved to the suburb of Porirua, north of Wellington, in New Zealand when he was young. Not only was he born and educated in two rugby heartlands, but among his cousins were Tana Umaga, who would be his captain in an All Blacks shirt, and Sinoti Sinoti, the Samoan International who played for Toulon and Newcastle, among others.

With rugby in his blood, and dominating physicality from a young age, he moved quickly through the New Zealand age grades. Aged 18, he led Northern United RFC, better known just as Norths, in Porirua, becoming the youngest captain of a senior club rugby team anywhere in the world. Collins was voted player of the tournament when the 'Baby Blacks' won the World Junior Championships in 1999. Within two years he was a regular for the Hurricanes in Wellington and became the first player from that U19 side to become a full All Black.

New Zealand rugby is not short of giants, but the 6' 3", 17st 2lb Collins, regularly sporting bleached blond hair, cut an imposing figure. He had the biggest biceps in the All Blacks squad, with a 52 cm circumference – the same size as Arnold Schwarzenegger at his peak of bodybuilding. So big were his 'pythons', he actually had to work to reduce their size when they began to interfere with his ability to tackle people properly.

His tackling was ferocious, and YouTube is full of clips of his 'greatest hits', with Colin Charvis, Sébastien Chabal, Thinus Delport and Nathan Sharpe among those starring in X-rated videos of their encounters with Collins.

In his autobiography, Tana Umaga explained the lengths to which opponents would go to avoid a close encounter with his cousin. "Players understand that when you're playing against Jerry Collins, you've always got to know where he is because you don't want to look up and find yourself carting the ball straight into his channel. Teams are good at making up plays that keep their ball-carriers away from him."[51]

The hit on Colin Charvis of Wales, during a 2003 fixture in Hamilton, was a particularly brutal collision. This ferocious moment in an altogether grisly afternoon for Wales, who lost 55-3, happened when the visitors were still just about holding their own. On 22 minutes, with the ball in midfield and the score just 7-3, Charvis took a quick ball at an angle and powered forward, aiming to punch a hole in the Kiwi defensive line. But waiting for him was his opposing No. 8, Collins, who not only smashed into Charvis, stopping the Swansea man in his tracks, but then pushed him back and, leaning in on him, basically folded him into the floor.

For those of you who can't recall, Charvis was 6' 3" and a stone heavier than Collins at 18st 2lbs, but his own physical attributes didn't stop him from being on the receiving end of a hard, but legal, Collins thunderbolt.

Charvis lay crumpled and unconscious on the pitch, but play continued as the All Blacks broke away and his desperate teammates tried to stop the counter-attack. Fortunately for the Welshman, Tana Umaga was looking at Charvis rather than the holes in the Welsh defence and ran over to him, cleared his breathing passage and placed him in the recovery position as the doctors ran onto the pitch.

"When I got knocked out, Tana was brilliant – I was unconscious but he rolled me over and ensured I didn't swallow my gum-shield," Charvis said, recalling the incident to a journalist a few years later.[52]

Charvis left the pitch, and was later diagnosed as suffering from whiplash. Soon his fragile Welsh teammates collapsed too, as a debutant Dan Carter pulled the strings for the All Blacks in midfield. But Umaga's act of concern following his cousin's smash resulted in him receiving an international fair play award, the Pierre de Coubertin medal, and an acknowledgement of thanks from the Welsh Rugby Union.

Another of the modern-era hard men of the game who came up against Collins and had the rare experience of being bounced back was South African flanker Schalk Burger.

He recalls facing off against Collins in that period. "So that was my job, back in the day – try to keep Jerry quiet, or try to intimidate him if you could. Look, this was a bloke who never backed down: he was one of those players who would grab a ball 50 yards back, look you in the face and basically say as he advanced, 'OK, let's see who is the bravest here.'"

Burger recalls the 2005 Tri Nations Test between the 'Boks and All Blacks at Newlands as a particularly physical match, with him and Collins going hammer and tongs at each other for the 80 minutes.

"I think Jerry had a few on me that day. But that was what it was like playing Jerry: there was just no backing down. If you were the type of opponent to back down, I think he would have lost respect for you. He wanted you to show your respect by taking him head-on. Jerry won most of those collisions throughout his career. He was a tough player but also an honest and true man."

The 86-cap Springbok added, "A couple of hard men come on the scene and make their presence felt for a little while, but Jerry was one of those who stood the test of time. If you were carrying the ball, you always felt he was hunting you down, that he was coming."[53]

Fellow hard man Sébastien Chabal (profiled later in the book) was another major victim of a Collins smash in a 2007 summer tour match. The man nicknamed 'the Caveman' came into the game with a big reputation, having broken All Black Ali Williams' jaw earlier in the tour, but was he put hard onto the floor by an even bigger hit in midfield. Watching the video, it is clear that Chabal can see Collins approaching and tries to release the ball, but has no luck and no escape. The bigger they come, the harder they fall!

Collins was named as All Black captain for two matches at the 2007 World Cup, standing in for regular Richie McCaw, but that quarter-final defeat to France would be the last of his 48 caps.

Next up came his cameo for Barnstaple seconds, the Barbarians and an appearance under an assumed name for an amateur rugby league team that his cousins and friends played for, which saw him rapped on knuckles by the authorities. In May 2008 he announced he was retiring from International rugby and headed to Europe to continue playing, joining Toulon for a year, then heading to south Wales to link up with the Ospreys.

The Ospreys at this time were still able to welcome players from the top tier of world rugby, but the arrival of a 28-year-old All Black, still in the prime of his playing career, was a major coup. He made an immediate impact, was voted Players' Player of the Year in his first season, and played in the team that won the inaugural PRO12 final away at Leinster.

Wales and Lions full back Lee Byrne was a teammate at the Ospreys and became a close friend of Jerry's during his time in south Wales.

Their first meeting might not have immediately marked them out as future pals, as Byrne recalled to me. "I was making my debut for Wales, against New Zealand in 2005 at the Millennium Stadium. I'd just come off the bench and got the ball off Stephen Jones for my first touch, then suddenly I was flat on my back! I'd been absolutely blindsided by Jerry. I was seeing stars as this scary-looking fella with the bleach-blond hair stood over me. I got up and he patted me on the head. 'Next time step, bro,' he said. I said, 'I ain't got a step, mate.' He laughed and ran off to tackle someone else.

"Then when he joined the club, it gave everyone a lift. Even the seasoned pros thought, 'Wow, that's Jerry Collins.' And everyone raised their game accordingly."

Byrne likened his tackling to a 'suplex' from the World Wrestling Federation, and although Collins was often very relaxed in training and the coaches never pushed him too hard, he was "like a machine" when on the pitch. In some ways he was a bit of a throwback to the amateur era.

The playing aspect aside, he became a cult hero in south Wales, relishing its social life and regularly visiting local rugby clubs across the region.

Byrne has fond memories of the big Kiwi's love of Wales. "There's loads of stories about him. On a Sunday he'd just rock up at random places. He'd have a look at a map of Wales and say to the taxi driver, 'Take me there.'"

There's one story that particularly stands out. "One Sunday he'd gone up to a village in the Swansea Valley and went into a pub to watch a match. He asked the barman where the TV was, but it was pretty small. So, he left the pub, got a taxi to Comet, bought a big TV there, came back to the pub with it under his arm, plugged it in, watched the game and then left it there. He was always very generous like that."

Another Byrne memory was formed on an early-morning stroll home from a nightclub. "A rubbish truck was doing its rounds and Jerry – who'd once been a binman in his home town of Wellington – decided he wanted to help. The next thing I knew, he was on the back of the truck, getting off to collect the rubbish bags. The crew didn't mind – they even let me sit up front with the driver."[54]

Leaving south Wales in 2011, his next stop was Yamaha Júbilo in Japan. Yamaha Rugby spokesman Jin Hasegawa said, "He was a great player and was very good with relating to the public. He was very polite and kind to the Japanese supporters and would sign his signature for them and shake their hand. He was a former All Black, so very popular."

But Collins' time in the land of the rising sun is best remembered for a bizarre incident that saw him arrested for carrying two knives in an upmarket department store. The police were called. One officer arrived and on taking one look at Collins, called for backup. And lots of it. Around 30 of Hamamatsu's finest flooded the store, surrounding Collins. But they needn't have worried: the man nicknamed 'the Terminator' had handed over the knives to a security guard before the police arrived, and came quietly.

News of Collins' arrest caused a major buzz in New Zealand, and there was a great deal of speculation as to what had actually happened. After 11 nights in jail, he was released and issued with a fine. He said he was carrying the knives in self-defence, after a 'misunderstanding' had led to several threats from a Brazilian biker gang who operated in the city. Whilst this might sound unlikely, the city of Hamamatsu has a significant Brazilian population and eventually his lawyer issued a statement saying the 'misunderstanding' might have been about a woman.

Not long after this incident, Collins departed Japan and took a break from the game. Always one to follow his own path, he headed to Grande Prairie, in Alberta, Canada. In this small city, he worked as a security contractor in the oil fields, for a firm owned by a fellow New Zealander. There were plenty of other Kiwis and Islanders to work alongside – including, for a time, former Samoa and Wasps star Trevor Leota. Collins enjoyed his two years in western Canada, still playing the odd game for recreation, before he was lured back into professional rugby, signing a short-term contract with Narbonne, in the French second division.

The coach of Narbonne was former Australian forward Justin Harrison, and the club was owned by another ex-Wallaby, Rocky Elsom. The addition of Collins made an immediate impact. When he arrived on the Mediterranean coast, they were in the relegation places and looking certainties for the drop, but a series of man-of-the-match performances from Collins and an unbeaten home record steered them up the table and into safety.

The Jerry Collins story would, however, have a sudden and tragic end.

He had met and married his wife, Alana Madill, whilst living in Canada and they were proud parents of a ten-week-old daughter, Ayla, when on the night of 5 June 2015, the family suffered a fatal road accident near Béziers in the south of France. Returning late at night from a function, their car veered across the road and into a barrier before being struck by a bus. Collins died protecting his daughter by throwing himself across her baby seat as the bus impacted. The driver of the bus pulled Ayla out of the wreckage, but no one else would survive the accident.

Alana Madill was 35. Jerry Collins was 34.

From Samoa to Swansea, from New Zealand to Narbonne and many, many places in between, the outpouring of shock and sadness at the tragedy and the love and respect for Jerry Collins was immense.

To pick just a few of the tweets that were posted in the immediate aftermath of the news breaking, a regular opponent in Tri Nations tussles, former Springbok captain John Smit, described him as "One of the toughest AB's [All Blacks] to have played against."

Scottish International Gregor Townsend had his own memory that would be familiar to many opponents: "One of the toughest men to play our game. Tried to tackle him in 2000 and ended up with a broken rib. RIP."

Welsh referee Nigel Owens added his condolences: "RIP Jerry Collins. Deepest sympathy to all concerned. Was a great player and always a pleasure to referee."

The New Zealand Rugby Union described him as "one of the toughest and most uncompromising forwards to ever play for the All Blacks and his ferocious tackling and intimidating presence made him feared by every opponent."

In the week following the tragedy, several former All Blacks playing in France performed a haka in tribute on the site of the accident. Around 3,000 people attended his public funeral in Porirua, where Collins' coffin was draped in his beloved Norths' blue and white colours. His first club then renamed their ground the Jerry Collins Stadium.

Collins' close friend and ex-All Black Chris Masoe spoke at the funeral, saying, "When you realised what was coming and you protected Ayla from the impact with your arms and your whole body over her... you made it possible for her to have a chance. That's the man you are."[55]

New Zealand legend Jonah Lomu, speaking to reporters after the funeral, said, "Listening to the reports and what they say about how they found him, that he was protecting his baby, that's just typical Jerry. You talk about laying your body on the line and he did that. You look at what kind of player he is and what kind of person he is, and he typified having heart and standing up for what he believed in but also having everybody's back."[56] Sadly, just six months after Collins' passing, it would be Jonah Lomu to whom the world of rugby would be paying tribute.

Later in 2015, after New Zealand had won the World Cup that had proved elusive to Collins' generation of All Blacks, members of the team brought the Webb Ellis Cup to his grave in Porirua.

The tributes continued to pour in and the global rugby community rallied round by fundraising for his daughter, who, though she suffered severe injuries, has recovered well and now lives with her mother's family in Canada, but has visited her late father's home in New Zealand. Ayla may never have got to know her father, but his immense legacy will live on.

Jerry Collins was a truly remarkable player, a hard nut who could make even the most adept of opponents doubt themselves. His shuddering tackles, huge hits and big smile, sometimes all at the same time, proved to be his trademark. He was fearless and brave, a trait that would ultimately save his daughter's life.

On and off the pitch, he would always make his presence felt; and in the time-honoured rugby tradition – which can sometimes stray into cliché, but in Collins' case was true – he'd brutally batter you for 80 minutes, then buy you a beer in the clubhouse afterwards. Whilst he was a professional-era player, I don't think he would have minded playing a decade or two earlier.

We can leave the final words with another great All Black flanker, Michael Jones, who described Collins as "One of the most unique rugby players in world rugby and one of the most unique characters."

Jones added, "He's definitely one of the most special players who will ever wear a black jersey... He took the No. 6 jersey to new dimensions. The game became a lot more physical and confrontational... His trademark was not just being physical but influential, and I think that's very much how he played the game and how he lived his life."[57]

Jones ended the interview by admitting relief that he had never faced Collins on the field as an opponent. That is perhaps the best tribute of all.

NORM HADLEY

"When Hadley finally stood up, he looked at me and asked, 'Is that all you've got, Princess?'"

"WHAT THIS COUNTRY needs is more Norman Hadleys!"

The words of Canadian rugby fans, ecstatic at their quarter-final appearance in the 1991 World Cup? No. Perhaps a plea from the team's management for more youngsters to eschew the puck and pick up an oval ball instead? No.

They are in fact the words of British Prime Minister John Major in the House of Commons in 1992. MPs on all sides of the chamber cheered him, one of the few times this happened in his difficult spell as leader.

His praising of the big Canadian was not because of anything he had done on the pitch, though he always impressed there too. Instead the commendation was for a few moments on the London Underground whilst Hadley was playing for Wasps.

He was sitting on the Tube when two youths began misbehaving. It began with bad language, then out came the cigarettes (just five years after 31 deaths in the Kings Cross inferno had led to a smoking ban across all areas of the Underground), and they got more abusive when asked by other passengers to stop. Enter Hadley, who was returning home from a day at work. How they hadn't clocked the 6' 7", 21-stone figure sitting in the carriage, we will never know. Maybe it wasn't tobacco they were smoking. But, raising himself up to his full height, Hadley strode over to the two troublemakers. It is easy to imagine his shadow falling across them before they looked up and saw they'd chosen the wrong carriage to irritate people in. As the train pulled into the next station and the doors opened, Hadley picked each one up in turn, took a few steps and deposited them on the platform. The doors closed. The stunned hoodlums were left behind. And the carriage burst into a round of applause as the train moved off and Hadley retook his seat and returned to his newspaper.

The press loved the story and it soon reached the corridors of power, where it particularly appealed to a Prime Minister who tried to talk tough on law and order. The hero of the story was bemused, remarking to a Canadian magazine, "I spent years playing high-level rugby and barely anyone knows me. I sort out yobs on the Tube and suddenly I'm famous around the globe."[58]

Norm Hadley was a key part of a golden era of Canadian rugby, the high point being their performance at the 1991 World Cup. In the group stage, they defeated both Romania (who were a formidable outfit in the early 1990s) and the ever-lively Fiji, and only a 19-13 defeat to France stopped them topping the group. Their tournament would end with a narrow quarter-final loss to New Zealand, where it is clear on the video highlights that the Maple Leaf forwards matched their more illustrious All Black counterparts and it was the backs that ultimately made the difference.[59]

Glenn Ennis, who played No. 8 for Canada at this tournament, told me more about what he believes made that team so special. "The golden age of Canadian rugby was all about a forward pack that was tough enough to say 'Fuck you' to any and all forward packs on the planet, and then back it up with hard play, or fists if needed. Norm was a perfect anchor to that pack. He was the biggest man in the 1991 World Cup, in the biggest forward pack, and not one of us would even think about pissing him off."

Sadly, Canada have never since reached such heights in the World Cup. When they played New Zealand in the 2019 edition, they lost 63-0, and in the same fixture at the 2011 tournament they suffered a 79-15 reverse.

World Rugby Hall of Fame member Al Charron, a teammate of Hadley's, remembered him fondly when he spoke to me. "Even as a youngster, he was a big boy – he was like a tree trunk. I remember standing next to him and being in his shadow! Although at this time we weren't meant to lift in the line-out, we still did, and boy was it tough to get him up in the air!

"He was a tough guy. Norm made all of us on the team feel bigger and braver when he was with us. He was also one of the wittiest guys I ever played with. Sure, he had a sharp tongue, but he would have us in stitches in the dressing room or on the bus."

Ennis adds to this: "Norm was a monster both on and off the field. And by monster, I mean he was a combination of things that scared everyone. He scared a lot of guys who thought they were big and tough, but his intellect was even more frightening. He was by far the cleverest person I've ever met. He was a full genius.

"I was in a lot of fights right by his side, on and off the field, and there was no one better to have beside you. But most of all I remember being beside him and laughing – he was an even more accomplished comedian than a fighter. He used his genius to make us all laugh."

Born in Winnipeg, a city far more famous for ice hockey than rugby, Hadley was unusual in his sport of choice. The heartlands of Canadian rugby lie in British Columbia, on the country's Pacific coast – although another hard man of the game, Jamie Cudmore, also calls 'the gateway to the west' home. Hadley played ice hockey as a youngster but would swap the puck for a ruck. "I grew too big to get drafted by a professional team. In retrospect, when I look at their salaries, I should have stayed with ice hockey."[60]

He may not have made the millions that a career in the NHL might have offered, but he had brains to match the brawn, earning a Bachelor of Economics degree from the University of Victoria and an MBA from the University of Columbia, and also gaining further professional qualifications at the London School of Economics.

His rugby career straddled the last days of the amateur era and the first blossoming of the paid game, so whilst he spent some time as a professional, most of his rugby was played while he was still pursuing a high-flying career in finance. He held roles at Cantor Fitzgerald, Barclays and last worked as managing director of Deutsche Bank in Tokyo, proving he was as successful with a spreadsheet or in a boardroom as he was in driving a maul or taking a line-out ball.

In Japan, he played for Suntory Sungoliath with Canada teammate Glenn Ennis, who recalls another incident highlighting Hadley's off-the-field toughness and honour code. "I was with Norm on the streets of Tokyo in the chaos of New Year's Eve, when a group of foreign guys (about ten of them) surrounded a couple of Japanese girls and began harassing and molesting them. We saw what was happening and went in fists flying. The girls got away, and we were walking back to the station when Norm stopped and said, 'I can't leave it at that.' He walked back a block, found the same bunch of guys and went crazy on them. I was right behind him but before I could even join in, six were on the ground and the rest ran off."

It's worth noting here that Ennis himself had a strong reputation on the pitch and has a particularly interesting post-rugby career. After a long stint playing in Japan, he has become a successful actor and stuntman in movies and television. His credits include *Watchmen*, *Deadpool*, *Justice League* and – perhaps most eye-catchingly – he played the bear that mauled Leonardo Di Caprio in the Oscar-winning *The Revenant*. After time learning about how bears moved and attacked, he donned a blue suit with a bear head to film the famous scene and CGI filled in the bear's likeness afterwards. Perhaps being at the coalface of rugby for so many years gave Ennis a little bit of inspiration.

The Canadian team built on their success at the 1991 World Cup, beating Wales, France and an England XV featuring the likes of Martin Johnson, Neil Back and Kyran Bracken in the years that followed. Hadley captained Canada when they ran a full England team close in a fixture in London in 1992, losing 26-13, and his performance was well remembered by England prop Jason Leonard.

"One of the England lads got on the wrong side of an early ruck, so Hadley decided to get him out of the way. I took huge exception to Hadley's method, so I threw one of the biggest punches of my life at him. He was bending down and my punch landed on his forehead. I thought, 'Well, that's you sorted.'"

Leonard, who won 114 caps for England during his 14-year International rugby career and was no stranger to some of the physical aspects of the game, had not, however, encountered anyone quite like Stormin' Norman!

"I just had not realised how big he was. He started to stand up, and it went on and on, so I had plenty of time to watch this egg-sized lump growing on his forehead. For my part, I had a dislocated finger. When Hadley finally stood up, he looked at me and asked, 'Is that all you've got, Princess?' He spent the rest of the match chasing me around the pitch. Fortunately, he never caught up with me."[61]

Eddie Evans played that day at prop for Canada and recalls the fixture well. "That was a real tough game. I had my hand broken in it. The shot that Jason put on Norm would have put down a large rhino. But not Norm! We all miss the big man. He was very articulate and educated, but on the pitch he was the complete opposite – the ultimate nightmare to play against!"

The same year he was chasing Leonard around the London turf – 1992 – Hadley was also selected for the Barbarians, against world champions Australia at Twickenham. It was a particularly strong Baa-Baas team; the other lock that day was All Black Ian Jones and the centre pairing was Will Carling and Scott Gibbs. Hadley would go on to represent the Barbarians four further times.

His strength and ability on the pitch, coupled with his size and strong opinions, made him a regular on the BBC's weekly *Rugby Special* programme, among others. In 1997 Britain's glossy *Total Sport* magazine named him in their special 'The Blood and Guts, Hard Issue' as one of the world's 12 toughest sportsmen.

His strident views on the game would, however, land him in difficulty. He was openly critical of the inability of the Canadian management to adapt to the new professional game and build on the promise of the 1991 World Cup. This dispute saw him miss the 1995 World Cup, where his team sorely missed him in a tough pool that included South Africa and Australia, and exited at the group stage. In part due to the distance between his home country and his work in London, and a lack of fixtures compared to the packed calendar now, Hadley – one of the true greats of Canadian rugby – only won 15 caps for his country between 1987 and 1994, five as captain.

The premature departure of Hadley and his athleticism and commitment from the International set-up was one of the reasons for the beginning of the slow descent of Canadian rugby. Post-1991 World Cup, there was some brief talk of Canada joining the Five Nations (as it was then) but that never went any further than speculation, with Italy finally getting the nod in 2000. Challenges in funding a professional sport also played a part, coupled with the decline of the amateur club scene, concerns over rising insurance costs and difficulty in keeping young talent flowing into the game when there are so many other sports and activities vying for their time. None of these are unique to Canada, but when the sport is only moderately popular, then they can be particularly biting.

Al Charron, who scored a famous try to defeat Wales at the old Cardiff Arms Park in 1993, sees finance as the big obstacle. "Professional rugby is great, but it hasn't helped Canada. I think in 1991 we could have done better; we were slow to get going versus France in the group and could have beaten them. We still had a chance of doing something at the 1995 Rugby World Cup, but after that we were slow to grasp the new era. It's much better now: we have many more structures, a team in Major League Rugby and our sevens and women's teams are doing well. But for the men's team, it's hard to surprise people – everyone now does their homework. It's tough to get a result against one of the big teams. But we keep working, and I still see some great opportunities out there."

Canada have not beaten a Tier One nation since a win over Argentina in 2005 and the recent World Cups have only underlined how far they now lag behind not only the major nations but also those teams that used to be regularly beaten by the Maple Leafs. The USA are now the number one North American team, and at the time of writing (June 2020), Canada lie 23rd in the world rankings, behind the likes of Hong Kong, Portugal and Russia.

So Hadley's sudden death from a heart attack in a Tokyo hotel room in March 2016, aged just 51, brought not just an outpouring of grief at the premature loss of such a powerful and popular character but also a harking back to a lost era of amateurism when Canada were a force to be reckoned with, whoever they were playing.

Hadley was a big man, with an even bigger legacy. His passing led to a deluge of anecdotes and fond memories from teammates and fans, even over 20 years after he'd stopped playing. A hard man on the pitch, and a robust character off it too, his combination of athleticism and intellect made him a remarkable figure.

I wouldn't be agreeing with John Major on much, but on Norm Hadley he was spot on.

DAVID BEDELL-SIVRIGHT

"When I go on to that field, I only see the ball,
and wherever it goes I go too, and should
someone be in the road, that is his own lookout."

FACTFILE

Full name: David Revell Bedell-Sivright

Born: 8 October 1880, Edinburgh, Scotland

Died: 5 September 1915, Gallipoli, Turkey

Position: Prop

Representative teams: Scotland, British & Irish Lions

Clubs: Cambridge University RUFC, Edinburgh University RFC, Fettesian-Lorettonian Club, Barbarians, West of Scotland FC, Edinburgh Wanderers RFC

Nickname: Darkie

WHEN YOU THINK of a classic hard man of rugby, who normally comes to mind? Perhaps a grizzled South African hammering into tackles? Maybe a Kiwi farmer, all elbows at the line-out. Or the Welsh steelworker or English policeman bringing a little of the toughness of their profession onto their field of play?

So, with these archetypes in mind, someone born into an upper-middle class Edinburgh family, educated at the fee-paying boarding school Fettes – nicknamed 'the Eton of the North' and the inspiration for J K Rowling's Hogwarts – before

Not just tough on the pitch: legendary Irish hard man Paddy Mayne with the SAS, North Africa, 1942

Brian Lima's huge tackle on Derick Hougaard during the Rugby World Cup match between South Africa and Samoa, 2003

A bloodied but unbowed Wayne
Shelford v. France, 1989

Mark Leech / Getty Images

One third of Max Boyce's renowned
'Pontypool Front Row': Bobby Windsor
v. Ireland

Huw Evans Picture Agency

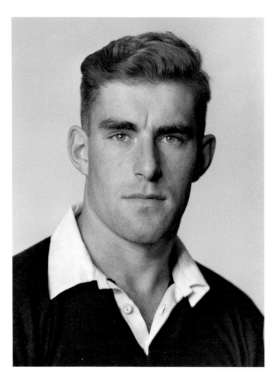

A giant of an All Black: Colin Meads, 1956

Jerry Collins just a month before his tragic death in 2015, playing for Narbonne v. Dax

Norm Hadley
powers forward
for Bedford v.
Bath,1995

Andrew Redington /
Getty Images

Notorious
carthorse
botherer David
Bedell-Sivright
lines up for
Scotland, circa
1904

Photographer
unknown / Public
domain

Scott Gibbs upends South Africa's Andre Snyman during the first Test of the 1997 Lions Tour

Some of the infamous French pack of the 1970s (L–R): Michel Palmié, Jean-Pierre Bastiat, Robert Paparemborde, Alain Paco, Gérard Cholley and Jean-Pierre Rives

Bakkies Botha squares up to Sam Whitelock of New Zealand, 2011

Phil Walter / Getty Images

Tomás Lavanini tussles
with Eben Etzebeth at the
2015 Rugby World Cup

Onside Images

Jacques Burger salutes
the fans after a victory for
Saracens, 2010

Captain of the only northern hemisphere team to lift the Rugby World Cup to date: Martin Johnson, Leicester v. Bath, 1996

You can see the awe on the young autograph hunter's face: a battle-scarred Brian Thomas in his playing days

Weary Dunlop (left) and Lt.-Col. Albert Coates at Nakhon Pathom hospital camp, Thailand post-liberation, reviewing sketches made by fellow POW Jack Chalker

heading south to study at Cambridge University and then commencing a career as a doctor, would on paper not perhaps strike you as likely to be a particularly tough rugby player. Perhaps that could be the CV of a certain type of winger, quick and elusive but not particularly interested in tackling and whose kit rarely got too muddy. Well, if so, you've clearly not met David Bedell-Sivright, who, whilst having the trappings of privilege, was as ferocious a player as you would be unlucky enough to face.

One of his contemporaries at Cambridge remembers his style: "He was always a very, very hard player, and took an absolute delight in the game... his great strength... made him a danger to the other side."[62]

Off the pitch too, he was notorious for his antics. There is a story about him that apparently happened after playing for Scotland and indulging in a particularly riotous night out in the Scottish capital. First he knocked out a carthorse with a single punch, then later in the evening he proceeded to lie down on a tram track on Princes Street, one of the major thoroughfares in central Edinburgh. The trams rolled to a halt and Bedell-Sivright relaxed for over an hour, either oblivious to or uncaring of the chaos this was causing. The police were called but, wary of his fiery reputation and mindful of their own safety, kept a respectful distance. Eventually, feeling suitably recharged, he got up and strolled off. Where he went is not recorded, but one would suspect it wasn't home to bed.

A handful on a night out, no doubt, but Bedell-Sivright was first and foremost a superb rugby player. He first played first-class rugby at Cambridge, where he participated in four Varsity matches against Oxford, and whilst still a student he made his Scotland debut against Wales in 1900. This would be the first of 22 caps, and he won three Triple Crowns (wins over Ireland, Wales and England in the same Championship) in 1901, 1903 and 1907. To this day, he remains the only Scot to have achieved this feat.

A powerful prop, he was famous for his enormous physicality during games. A Scotland teammate of his, Andrew 'Jock' Wemyss, described him as "one of the many great forwards of the early century... a very, very hard player of immense strength whose fiery determination on the field often led to the accusation he was 'over-zealous'."[63] And Wemyss knew a little about determination: he lost an eye in World War I, but that didn't get in the way of him returning to the Scottish International team once hostilities were over.

It seems that Bedell-Sivright agreed with his teammate's assessment, stating, "When I go on to that field I only see the ball, and wherever it goes I go too, and should someone be in the road, that is his own lookout."[64]

In 1903 he was selected for the Lions tour of South Africa, but injury saw him fail to play in any of the Tests. The first two were drawn and the visitors succumbed in the final fixture to lose the series 1-0. The Lions' touring schedule in Edwardian times was a very different proposition to today's highly regimented set-up, and just a year later they were off again, this time to Australia and New Zealand. Bedell-Sivright was again selected – the only player kept on from the previous tour – and this time, despite being just 24, he was named captain.

Clem Thomas, himself a Lion in 1955 before becoming a renowned rugby writer, wrote glowingly of Bedell-Sivright in his seminal history of the Lions. "Apparently he was a man after my own heart, being a rough handful as a player. He was one of the first in a long line of Scottish forwards to master the art of wing-forward play, and had the reputation of breaking up opposing teams with his marauding spoiling."[65]

Thomas, let us remember, in addition to spending 35 years writing for *The Observer*, was also a wholesale butcher, and was sometimes accused by opponents of bringing his professional skills onto the field of play.

Under Bedell-Sivright's leadership, the Lions won all 14 of their matches on the Australia leg of the tour, scoring 265 points and conceding just 51. This run of victories included three comprehensive triumphs over the national team. Bedell-Sivright's captaincy was always forthright. In one game the tourists had been having an ongoing dispute with a local referee, Hugh Dolan, who eventually sent off one of the Lions – English winger Denys Dobson – who he claimed had "personally insulted" him. Bedell-Sivright was not playing in this particular match but waded into proceedings, pulling the team off the pitch for 20 minutes whilst he argued with the referee and local officials. The Lions eventually returned to the field without Dobson and, despite being a man short, won 17-3.

After the match, Bedell-Sivright explained his actions to one journalist, who reported: "He regarded the referee's charges as a personal insult, not only to Mr Dobson, but to the whole of the members of the team. The alleged offence was not any breach of the rules of the game, but a personal one, which would reflect on the character of anyone guilty of it and through him on the whole of his comrades."[66]

A clearly exasperated Bedell-Sivright added that he could not believe that Oxford-educated England International Dobson, who he referred to as "one of the quietest and most gentlemanly members of the team", could be guilty of what he had been accused of by Dolan, and pointed out that the referee had had his back to the players at the time and had sent Dobson off without making any inquiries into who had said what to whom.

Eventually an enquiry cleared Dobson of using indecent language but found him guilty of using "an improper expression" and of directing this at the referee, although it was decided no further action would be taken. No action was taken against Bedell-Sivright either. You are surely wondering what the expression was that caused such a fuss. Well, it was not officially confirmed, but local papers reported it as: "What the devil was that for?"

Mr Dolan must have been a very sensitive soul indeed.

As an aside, Dobson, a career civil servant in the Colonial Office, was, once his rugby career had finished, posted to Nyasaland (today known as Malawi), where in 1916 he died after being fatally gored by a charging rhinoceros. When news of his death reached England, a former contemporary from his Oxford playing days cruelly remarked that he "...always had a weak hand-off."

The five-match New Zealand leg of the tour was far less successful for the Lions. Bedell-Sivright broke his leg in the first match, and they lost the sole Test against the All Blacks 9-3. The captain's absence, it was said, had a big impact on the team's performance.

Whilst the tour ultimately ended in failure, Bedell-Sivright was so enamoured with Australia that he stayed on afterwards, recuperating from his injury and then working as a jackaroo on a cattle station before taking the boat home to complete his medical studies in Edinburgh. Fortunately he had suffered no lasting damage to his leg and once home, he captained Edinburgh RFC and returned to the Scottish national team. He was in the team that beat South Africa 6-0 at Hampden Park in 1906, the last Home Nations team to defeat South Africa for nearly 60 years, and he became the first British or Irish player to play a Test match against each of Australia, New Zealand, and South Africa.

He retired from International rugby in 1908, but soon began channelling his aggression elsewhere and within a year had become Scottish amateur heavyweight champion. A report on his lifting the belt said he had won "not by particularly scientific boxing but by hard punching."[67]

Medical practice and club rugby filled the next few years, before World War I began and he immediately volunteered for the Royal Navy as a surgeon. In 1915 he was posted to Gallipoli in Turkey with the Royal Marine Light Infantry, serving onshore in a field hospital in the trenches. There, it was a mosquito rather than a bullet or a bomb that felled one of rugby's hardest men. Complaining of fatigue, he was taken to a hospital ship, where on 5 September he died of septicaemia and was buried at sea off Cape Helles. It was the same cause in the same Dardanelles campaign that had accounted for another decent rugby player, the poet Rupert Brooke, a few months earlier.

Sadly, Surgeon David Bedell-Sivright Medical Unit, R.N. Div., Royal Navy was one of all too many rugby players who both played and died for their country. A total of 140 International players were killed in World War I. The losses the sport felt were, like all those in the war, devastating. To give just a small indication, of the 30 men that played in Scotland's 16-15 defeat to England in March 1914, 11 would not survive the conflict – one of those lost being the Scottish captain that day, Eric Milroy, who as a lieutenant in the Black Watch was killed at the Battle of the Somme just two years later.

When Bedell-Sivright died, *The Referee*, a newspaper published in Sydney, Australia, wrote of the news: "It is cabled that Dr D. R. Bedell-Sivright, who captained the British team in Australia and New Zealand in 1904, has died at the Dardanelles... Sivright was a Scottish forward of the most brilliant type, a hard player, but a clever one. He was one of the finest all-round forwards ever seen in Australia from over the seas. Among the forwards of the teams since 1899, he divided honours with A. F. Harding, the famous Welshman, and, at his best, was fit for a world's team. Sivright as captain was somewhat dour, but as [a] player he was magnificent. A man of superb physique, it is hard to think that he has died an ordinary death at his age, and not to a bullet from the enemy."[68]

The respect they pay him is clear.

Gone but not forgotten, Bedell-Sivright's name and reputation has lived on. Writing in 1919 in his memorial of lost players, E H D Sewell spoke very highly of him: "If a plebiscite was taken on the question: 'Who was the hardest forward who ever played International football?' Sivright would get most votes if the voting was confined to players, and probably so in any event."[69]

Edinburgh University RFC give an annual scholarship in Bedell-Sivright's honour stating, "His memory lives on through this club, and we honour his commitment, passion for the game and compassion for humanity through our scholarship fund for talented young rugby players. Even though he was greatly feared in the ring and on the pitch, he upheld great sportsmanship, an attribute we regard as most important."[70]

He was an inaugural inductee into the Scottish Rugby Hall of Fame in 2010, and three years later was inducted into the International Rugby Board (now World Rugby) Hall of Fame.

Quite what the taciturn, brooding Scot would make of such honours, we will never know. But for his success in leading Scotland and the Lions, his dynamic forward play, not to mention his fearsome reputation, off-the-pitch antics, and in the end making the ultimate sacrifice in conflict, Bedell-Sivright is a very worthy member of our own particular hall of fame.

SCOTT GIBBS

"I didn't feel a thing, but it obviously hurt him."

JACOBUS PETRUS DU RANDT, better known as 'Os' (the Afrikaans for 'ox'), is a true South African rugby icon. The loose-head prop became the first Springbok to win two World Cups (1995 and 2007), his 80 caps saw him retire as the most-capped forward in the national team's history and coming in at 6' 3" and 21 stone, his physicality ensured dominance in the scrum as well as regular bullocking runs in open play. He has a personality nearly as big as he is and isn't a man to take things lying down. Except, that is, on 28 June 1997, when he came face to face with Scott Gibbs in a collision still talked about to this day.

The venue was Newlands, Cape Town. The event was the first Test between South Africa and the British & Irish Lions. It was du Randt v. Gibbs. Welsh v. Afrikaans rugby cultures.

An irresistible force versus an immovable object. But it was du Randt who ended up on the floor seeing stars.

But let's rewind a moment. A Lions tour is always a special event, but there was a particular magic about the 1997 tour to South Africa. The sporting wilderness created by apartheid meant it was the first time the best of the UK and Ireland had faced off against the Springboks since 1980. It was the inaugural Lions tour of rugby union's professional era. There have always been challenges around Lions tours – cost, player availability, blending national teams, disruptions to professional and personal life brought about by being away from home for so long, to name but a few. But the brave new world of players being paid, combined with the solidification of the World Cup as the new peak of rugby competition in the calendar, all cast doubt on the continuation of the tours.

Former Lions player and 1997 team manager Fran Cotton summed up some of the pre-tour concerns: "The first professional Lions had been written off as 'no hopers' before they left for South Africa, and the very future of Lions tours was being questioned by people with their own selfish, commercial axes to grind."[71]

And then there was the opposition. The team the Lions would be facing were world champions and confidence was high that the tourists wouldn't prove too tough as opponents. Louis Luyt, the South African Rugby Football Union president, stated at the start of the tour that the Lions were basically there to make up the numbers. Local sports magazine *SA Sports Illustrated*, in their pre-tour editorial, stated: "The British Lions arrived in South Africa rated – by their own media, South African media and supporters – as nothing more than rank underdogs. A nice bunch of blokes who were making a bit of history and, in so doing, winning friends rather than matches."

So whichever angle you took, there was a LOT for the Lions to prove on this tour.

And this collision was the defining moment.

The first Test was a tight, fractious affair which the Lions edged 25-16, and the second saw more of the same. The Lions led 6-5 at half-time, but shortly after the restart Percy Montgomery went over between the posts for South Africa and the momentum seemed to be swinging towards the home team.

Enter Scott Gibbs.

A scrum in midfield saw fly half Gregor Townsend receive the ball and slip it across to Gibbs. He ran a direct line through the South African defence then veered off ever so slightly, straight towards du Randt. The big Afrikaner tilted his body towards the approaching Welshman and had both arms out ready to stop the player in his tracks and wrap him up, as he had done countless times before. But this time it was different. Du Randt was hit so hard that it was him that was knocked back onto the floor. Gibbs spun out of his attempted tackle and evaded another Springbok before offloading. A roar went around the ground, largely of amazement that du Randt had been sat down so forcefully. From the ruck that formed after Gibbs' break, the Lions won a penalty and never looked back, winning the game 18-15 and securing a series victory.

Scott Gibbs in his 2000 autobiography, aptly named *Getting Physical*, offers his view of the moment. "People have said that I could have side-stepped him, but I couldn't. If I'd been a few more yards away, I could have edged out and offloaded the ball before the tackle, but he was right in front of me. I hit him full on and must have caught him in a soft spot because he just collapsed on the deck and started moaning. I didn't feel a thing, but it obviously hurt him."[72]

That moment clearly made a big impression on Gibbs' centre partner that day, Jeremy Guscott. "Gibbsy wanted to take on the Springboks all by himself. He was so pumped up, he wanted to smash anything in a green jersey... He's not the biggest bloke in the world, but he would have taken on anyone that day. He was some player to have alongside you. When he made the break and thundered into Os du Randt, leaving du

Randt on the floor and spinning off to carry the ball again, it was one of the most inspiring moments I've ever experienced on a rugby field."[73]

A slightly rueful du Randt, interviewed years later for a documentary, offered his view (from what he can remember): "He was a big lad, and *ja*, definitely a strong runner. And if you don't size him up properly and if you get him in from the blind, it's hard to take him down."[74]

In a career strewn with big moments for Gibbs, this instance of extreme physicality looms large in rugby fans' memories. Gibbs himself commented, "It obviously made an impact on the people who saw it too, because so many now come up to me and want to talk about it. Perhaps that moment lifted the guys but you don't really know at the time. Certainly no one came up to me and gave me a pat on the back. It was just another small victory over the South Africans, another one biting the dust."[75]

This modest but confident view is a neat insight into the character of Gibbs – a man who, despite so many public moments, remains something of an enigma.

He was born in Pencoed, a hotbed of Welsh rugby talent on the outskirts of Bridgend which has produced the likes of fellow Lions Gareth Thomas, Gavin Henson and Gareth Cooper. After a few games for Bridgend and representing Wales Youth, he signed for Neath and made his debut on 22 September 1990 against Abertillery, in the centre alongside Allan Bateman, who would also be a Lions tourist in 1997.

Remarkably, after just ten games for the 'Welsh All Blacks', he received an International call-up and started against England in the Five Nations (as it was then) opener. He was on the losing side that day, but Gibbs' attitude to the game was clear even from that early stage, as he recalls in his autobiography. "Anytime anyone ran at me, I put them down, and I was in Carling [Will, England captain]'s face all the time."[76]

Not one to be overawed by his debut!

In 1991 he represented Wales at the World Cup, facing off against fellow hard man Brian Lima (profiled earlier in the book) in a group-stage defeat by Western Samoa in Cardiff. If truth be told, the last years of amateurism weren't kind to Welsh rugby – poor management from the WRU, some archaic approaches to training and selection, an exodus of players to rugby league and a decade-long hangover from the glory days of the Seventies all meant that Gibbs experienced more losses than wins in the national shirt during this period.

But whilst Wales were in the doldrums, Gibbs' reputation thrived and in 1992, fed up with what he saw as stagnation at Neath, he took the short trip down the A483 to join Swansea RFC. He scored a hat-trick of tries on his debut against Cardiff, and won the Welsh Championship in his first season.

A controversial move at the time, in his book he describes it with typical candour. "Whereas Neath spent so much time slogging away in training with not a rugby ball in sight, at Swansea they were really into playing football and the players had a lot more footballing ability. We did a lot of skills and drills in training and a lot less conditioning. I found that almost overnight I became a better player."[77]

One of the highlights of Gibbs' early-1990s spell at Swansea was something that would be almost inconceivable now – a club-team victory over a major International side. Yet this was what happened on a wet and windy Wednesday afternoon in November 1992, when world champions Australia came to Swansea's St Helens ground.

The visiting team, packed with the likes of John Eales, Tim Horan and Phil Kearns, couldn't handle the cold weather and red-hot atmosphere and the All Whites ran out 21-6 winners, with Gibbs – as ever – unstoppable from a few yards out, crashing over for the first try on what became a famous day for the old club. The BBC commentator on the match said that sort of try would be "his meal ticket for quite some time". He was right, but it would soon be rugby league, rather than union, that would be benefitting from Gibbs' potent mix of power and speed.

Whilst he had some major highlights with the All Whites and was selected for the Lions tour of New Zealand in 1993, where he made the starting XV for the second and third Tests, rugby union was still amateur. To make a living from it, rugby league was the only option. But it wasn't just a financial move for Gibbs. He'd already played in a World Cup, gone on a Lions tour, won domestic trophies with his club and was still only 24. For a man who sets high standards for himself and those around him, the professionalism of the league game, of which he'd been a fan since childhood, proved enticing. In the summer of 1994 he moved from the St Helen's ground of Swansea RFC to rugby league giants St Helens on Merseyside.

When Gibbs took the plunge, the road from Welsh union to English league was a well-trodden one. Jonathan 'Jiffy' Davies was perhaps the most well-known player to have made the move, but many of Gibbs' former teammates, like Scott Quinnell, Richard Webster and Dai Young, went at around the same time. For rugby fans during this time, rugby league seemed to loom like a bogeyman over the Welsh club game – except rather than punishing you for being naughty, it rewarded you for being very good. Watching the Challenge Cup on the BBC, the shoulder padding, shirts covered in sponsors' logos and matches played in front of raucous crowds in unfamiliar places like Wigan and Castleford gave the game an exotic sheen. The difference between the codes seemed to be far greater than just the rules and scoring; it was a completely different culture.

On signing, Gibbs told *The Independent*, "Rugby league is one of the toughest games on earth and I know that the physical demands are going to be very tough. But with the right conditioning and the right approach and attitude, I'm sure I can fit in."[78]

Fit in he did, and from the very start he wanted to show that his hard-man reputation gained in union also applied in league.

On his debut, in a friendly against Widnes, he wanted to put himself to the test. "I picked the biggest bastard on their side, who just happened to be a Tongan prop called Lee Hansen, and ran at him. After the game the boys said, 'Gibbsy, don't run at the big guys, especially not the likes of Lee Hansen,' but I didn't have a problem with it. I didn't get hurt."[79]

He stood up to the challenges of rugby league and became a better player. The more focused training and gym sessions meant he increased his weight by nearly three stone, and his chest and neck widened too, as the photos of him pre- and post- his rugby league debut prove.

Direct physical confrontation was a bigger part of the league game than union, and he relished the challenge. With his skills, focus and honed physique, the trophies duly followed, as he won both the Super League Championship and the Challenge Cup, as well as representing Wales at the Rugby League World Cup in 1995.

But even one of Wales' best rugby exports couldn't resist the lure of home for too long and in the summer of 1996, he re-signed with Swansea RFC. The game he was returning to was different to the one he had left – it was now officially professional, although with it still being in a period of transition, most players still held down regular jobs. A full-time contract was offered to Gibbs, and the lure of potential inclusion in the Lions tour to South Africa the following year made a return to the 15-man game impossible to turn down.

He was quickly back in the Wales squad, partnering again with Allan Bateman, who had also taken the return journey from league. Gibbs was thriving at an ebullient Swansea, and although the national team continued to struggle, his performances were enough to see him selected for his second Lions tour.

Gibbs' thunderous hit on Os du Randt is his best-known contribution to the success of the 1997 tour, but this does him a disservice. The 1997 Lions coach, Sir Ian McGeechan, described Gibbs as being "magnificent" on the tour and his hit on du Randt as a "seminal Lions moment".[80] In an intense battle for the centre positions, he saw off competition from Alan Tait and Will Greenwood for the No. 12 jersey and was voted 'Man of the Series'.

A fellow former rugby league star on the tour, John Bentley, himself no shrinking violet on or off the pitch, spoke highly of his fellow back. "Scott Gibbs used to intimidate his opposite number. They'd be lined up for a scrum or a line-out and he'd be shouting at their inside centre, 'I'm going to get you, I'm going to rip you apart,' and the rest of the team lifted, because he was on their side."[81]

For most rugby fans, it is Lions heroics for which Gibbs is best known, but in Wales it will always be a few moments of precision, skill and speed rather than blunt physical force for which he is most fondly remembered.

At the end of the 1990s, the Welsh national team had benefited greatly not just from the return of rugby league exiles, but also the welcoming of Graham Henry as coach. Upon being overlooked for the All Blacks coaching position, the New Zealander joined Wales, becoming the highest paid rugby union coach in the world, on a reputed £250,000 per year. Perhaps his nickname 'the Great Redeemer' was a little premature, but he brought a seriousness and professionalism, not to mention a few fellow Kiwis with Welsh ancestry (or not, as it turned out...) to the national team and guided them to 11 consecutive victories in 1999.

The standout triumph in this run was the win over England in the last ever match in the Five Nations, on 11 April 1999. Held at Wembley as the Millennium Stadium was still under construction, there were three minutes to go and with Wales losing 31-25, white ribbons were being tied to the trophy as England headed for a Grand Slam.

Many of you will remember the try. Wales line-out. Garin Jenkins threw in, Chris Wyatt took the ball off the top – just –

and dropped it into the hands of Rob Howley, who passed to the waiting Scott Quinnell. After a little juggle, he slipped the ball to an onrushing Gibbs, 30 metres out from the try line.

"Scott [Quinnell] and I called a move we had never practised," recalls Gibbs. "We'd both returned from rugby league and during the week I had talked about a play we used at St Helens that the scrum half Bobbie Goulding used a lot. The forwards would pack the midfield and he would run across, showing the ball to the opposition before slipping a short pass to someone bursting up.

"It was often devastating. I devised a version of our own when Scott would get the ball, run across the field, taking defenders with him, and I would come charging through at an angle, take a short pass and blast through the defence. We talked about it but never rehearsed it. We were all knackered when it came to that line-out and I told Scott to call it."[82]

He did, and it couldn't have worked better. On receiving the ball, at a sharp angle, Gibbs stepped to the right, then straightened up through Tim Rodber's attempted challenge, danced over a Neil Back ankle tap, swerved past England full back Matt Perry, leaving just Steve Hanley to try and stop him. Facing such speed and momentum, he had no chance and didn't even lay a hand on the Welsh centre as he went over. Neil Jenkins kicked the extras, Wales won 32-31, and England's capitulation saw the Championship go to Scotland.

The du Randt tackle and the Wembley try – two golden moments, two years apart but wonderful examples of rugby's various skills. Few players could put down 'the Bull' and waltz through a top-class defence, but Gibbs could.

Within two years of Wembley he had retired from International rugby, but not before being part of another World Cup and, although not named in the initial squad, he was an injury call-up for the Lions in 2001, his third tour with the elite of British and Irish rugby. In 2004 Gibbs retired completely, at the aged of 33. The final years of his club career spanned the disintegration of the Welsh club game and the move into the regional set-up. He was the last captain of the pre-regional Swansea RFC and the first of the Neath-Swansea Ospreys (now simply known as the Ospreys). Since retiring, he has studied business at university in the USA, lived in Italy and now calls South Africa home.

Scott Gibbs was always something of an enigma as a player, hard and uncompromising on the pitch, and certainly not opposed to some old-fashioned team bonding with a few beers. He was always honest in interviews – maybe too honest. Perhaps his most famous post-match comments came following Swansea's 37-10 win over Llanelli in the 1999 Welsh Cup Final, where he described the contest as "men against boys". A verdict, from my own recollection, delivered whilst dressed in just a towel outside the changing room.

Whilst always good for copy, he could be elusive for journalists, such was his tendency to quickly shower and hop in the car within minutes of a game. The car park outside Swansea's St Helen's ground was often the best place to guarantee catching a post-match quote from Gibbs. Off the pitch, his other passion is jazz – his biography is probably the only rugby one to mention both Buddy Rich and Steve Gadd.

The boy from Pencoed made a big impact, wherever he played. But let's give the final word to not just another Welsh rugby legend, but its greatest ever: Gareth Edwards, who in recalling Gibbs' 1997 Lions tour stated, "He frightened the Springboks. Hardness and physical impact is something they pride themselves on, but he beat them at their own game. In fact, he destroyed them."[83]

GÉRARD CHOLLEY

"He was like a huge nightclub bouncer going to work and you couldn't take your eyes off him for 80 minutes, he was always up to no good."

'THIS VIDEO MAY be inappropriate for some users.'

The warning flashed up on my laptop as I clicked on a video. I checked if my toddler was paying attention to what I was doing. She wasn't, so I clicked OK. Images filled the screen and I was transfixed. I became completely entranced by what I was watching, so when a small confused voice asked, "What's that, Daddy?", I was momentarily startled. I hadn't heard my daughter put down her dolls and wander over to the kitchen table. Suddenly she was there, staring at the images flickering on the screen too.

For a moment I didn't know what to say. What she was seeing was clearly adult material.

I had to be honest with her. I put my hand on her shoulder and told her it was rugby, but not normal rugby, French rugby from the 1970s. The game all looks the same to her, so she didn't register one moustachioed prop pummelling another into the ground in a muddy field in Béziers. She wrinkled her nose and returned to her doll's house and I continued to watch the video, despite YouTube's warning.

"I have seen pictures I never wanted to see again," said Serge Blanco, the French legend, in reference to the rugby he played in the 1970s. In the era of brutality, few could compete with the French, and whilst there was stiff competition as to who was the most fearsome figure to grace a *les Bleus* shirt in this period, the honour has to go to Gérard Cholley, who came in at 6' 4" and 20 stone and intimidated even the other fêted tough guys of this era.

Born at the very end of the Second World War in Fontaine-lès-Luxeuil in the east of France, he came late to rugby, not making his International debut until he was 30. He had been honing his skills and his physicality first in the French military, serving with the elite 8th Marine Infantry Parachute Regiment, then as a talented amateur boxer, and finally at the sharp end of club rugby.

There are plenty of stories about Cholley, and it is tempting to recount them all, including the one about how he discovered rugby. One Saturday night he was the last man standing after a bar brawl. Once the last punch had been thrown and the final chairs broken, the president of the local rugby club, who had been watching the chaos unfold, strode over and told Cholley, 'I want to buy you out of the Army. If you do this in a bar, I need you on the pitch for me.'

This, however, isn't true.

Not being from the heartlands of French rugby in the south-west of the country, his entry into the sport was far more prosaic than the bar-brawl myth, as he recounted to *Rugby World* in 2016.

"In my last month of service [1965] I went into a café in Castres, which was the seat of the rugby club. At that point in my life I'd never seen a rugby match, never even picked up a ball. The café owner looked at me and said, 'You're a big lad, you should be playing rugby.'

"The following Sunday, I went back to the same café for a coffee after lunch at the [army] canteen and the bus with the reserve team was just about to leave to play an away match. I decided to go with them to watch, and they talked me into playing even though I knew nothing about rugby. But during the match a fight broke out, and, well, I knew a lot about fighting. And I thought, 'This is the sport for me.'

"As it was the last month of my military service, I could do what I wanted in the evening, so the following week I trained every night and on Sunday I played again with the reserve team. Within a fortnight I was playing for the 1st XV."[84]

This was Castres Olympique, the grand old French club which he would represent for the next 15 years.

Whilst a punch-up in a pub might not have marked his entry into rugby, once he was playing, he quickly made his presence felt. In the first years of his club career, he was a second row, but it was only when he moved to prop that he made the step up to International class. He made the first of his 31 appearances for the national team in a victory over England at Twickenham in 1975, a game in which fellow French cult hero Jean-Pierre Rives also made his debut.

An opponent that day was England front row Fran Cotton, himself no stranger to some of the dark arts of the scrum, and he vividly recalls the unique challenge that the French – and in particular, Cholley – presented. "The French pack of the late 1970s was the scariest set of hombres I have encountered on a rugby pitch. There was Gérard Cholley on the loose head, who was absolutely massive. He was like a huge nightclub bouncer going to work and you couldn't take your eyes off him for 80 minutes, he was always up to no good."[85]

The most intense rivalry in the mid to late 1970s was between France and Wales. Cholley was a part of the 1977 Grand Slam team that prevented a fifth consecutive Welsh Championship win. France's feat was more remarkable as they did it with the same 15 players in all four matches (unique for a Grand Slam winner) and without conceding a try.

As detailed elsewhere in this book, Wales weren't putting choirboys in their front row but even they found Cholley's France hard to handle. As fellow hard man Bobby Windsor (profiled earlier in the book) recalls, "I played against France five times and had my nose broken five times."

Reeling off the eight names of the French pack – Alain Paco, Robert Paparemborde, Michel Palmié, Alain Estève, Jean-Pierre Rives, Jean-Claude Skrela, Jean-Pierre Bastiat and of course Cholley – Windsor adds: "That is going to be put on my headstone. It was like facing the A-Team. You had to fight fire with fire. If you got away 50-50 you had done well."[86]

Windsor's front-row colleague Charlie Faulkner has a similar recollection of those Gallic battles. "Pricey [Graham Price] had his eyes gouged by Cholley." Though Faulkner neglects to say how Price got his revenge, by biting his opponent's thumb. "You had to give some back against France. If you didn't retaliate or hold your own, they would walk all over you and give you a good kicking while they did."[87]

That 1977 Grand Slam also included a 23-3 win over Scotland in Paris – a match, however, best remembered for Cholley laying out four Scots. Footage of this match is hard to find, but I managed to track down some short clips.[88] The first Scot downed was their No. 8, Donald Macdonald, clocked with a right hook from behind at a maul. Minutes later, Ron Wilson tried to stop a bullocking run from Cholley but before he could, he was hit in the face by a fist that was preceding the Frenchman. The referee blew for a foul, and Cholley looked genuinely shocked to be penalised. He may have honestly thought it was a legal hand-off!

Ian Barnes, at lock for Scotland that day, recalls the prelude to the game, "I was rooming with [prop and future captain] Jim Aitken. He said to me, 'I don't think this guy Cholley is as hard as everyone makes out – first scrum, we will both hit him.' Now, I wasn't very keen on this idea but I was not going to let Jim know that, so I just kept quiet."

Barnes continued, "At the first scrum, I hit Cholley... Aitken didn't... Cholley exploded... fists flying everywhere. I was trying to keep him away with little pokes... I spent the next hour and a half avoiding Cholley – and that is a fair old trick in front of 70,000 people without anybody noticing."

Barnes doesn't pull any punches on who he had come up against that day. "He [Cholley] looked like Moby Dick in a goldfish bowl... If he had gone down a dark alley with King Kong, only one would have come out the other end – and it wouldn't have been the monkey!"[89]

During that same eventful tournament, whilst Cholley was psyching himself up before the fixture against Ireland at Lansdowne Road, he punched the ceiling in the changing room so hard it went through to the timber. His hand swelled to the size of a small melon, but he still took the field and France won 15-6.

Cholley's actions in 1977 haunted Scotland when they revisited Paris two years later.

"I was pretty apprehensive," says Iain Milne, Scotland's tight-head prop that day. "Not scared, but wary. I remember standing at the tunnel in Paris and looking at Cholley and the rest of them and they were like a gang of people who'd just been released from the Bastille prison. Then I looked at our lads – Ian McGeechan, Andy Irvine and Alan Lawson, with their beautiful combed hair and their white shorts – and I said, 'How are we going to survive this?'"[90]

Cholley took his brand of rugby brutality global, being selected for French tours in South Africa (1975), the United States (1976) and Argentina (1977). When one of his teammates was struck in a match against Western Province in South Africa, Cholley took justice into his own hands and knocked out three of his opponents.

Visitors from the southern hemisphere were given similar treatment. Gary Knight of New Zealand would win the first of 36 International caps against France in 1977 and Cholley almost blinded him by poking both his eyes after a line-out, leaving him with a torn eyelid.

Another All Black debutant that day, Gary Seear, remembers the shock of the treatment the French gave them. "I'd been to South Africa and had experienced a fair bit of physicality, so I knew about that side of it, but standing in the tunnel waiting to go out for my first Test... we were there for about five minutes and here's Gérard Cholley punching the walls. I thought, 'Jeez, so this is Test rugby.'"[91]

A late starter to International rugby, Cholley won his last cap in 1979 but would continue to be a stalwart for Castres for many more seasons. When he finally retired from the club game in 1980 he was honoured for his immense contribution to French rugby with a testimonial, attended by several of his former Welsh opponents, who reminisced long into the night. Cholley donated all the money raised by the event to a mental health charity.

His reputation for brutality did little to lower his standing in French rugby; indeed it helped secure a nice little sideline – supplementing his regular job as a potato farmer – as a chauffeur-cum-bodyguard for senior government officials. He remains a vice-president of Castres and in 2017 he was made a *Chevalier* (knight) of the Legion of Honour – the highest French order of merit.

The fact that he only terrorised International opponents for four years will have given many a blessed relief. An immensely powerful player – he'd be big even now, and this was long before weight training and gyms – his physique was matched with a mean streak that emerged when he pulled on his boots.

Off the pitch he proved to be an avuncular and popular figure – the French team of this period were renowned for brutalising opponents in the afternoon and then ensuring they saw the very best bars and clubs that night, and Cholley embraced this approach to the game.

Rugby in France has a huge focus on local pride; unlike the other nations in the Six Nations, most fans put their club's interests ahead of the country's. There's a phrase that is used to illustrate this, *L'esprit de clocher* (literally 'the spirit of the belltower'), which manifests itself in an immense pride in home, but also a mistrust and opposition of 'the other', even if that's aimed at those just a few miles down the road. Cholley, in his fanatical commitment to his own team's fortunes, and disregard for his opponent's safety (often as well as his own), is an extension of this particularly Gallic brand of provincialism.

We'll give the final word to Cholley's old sparring partner and fellow hard man Bobby Windsor, who voted him into his all-time XV: "You've got to go a bit to be voted the most feared man in French rugby, but he managed it without breaking too much sweat. A fearsome bloke with a neck the size of an Aberdeen Angus bull... he played in the best pack I ever came up against. Definitely the sort of player you'd rather have on your side, if only because you'd save yourself a lot of aggro!"[92]

TREVOR BRENNAN

"I did my usual double act –
sin-binned and Man of the Match."

FACTFILE

Full name: Trevor Brennan

Born: 22 September 1973, Dublin, Republic of Ireland

Positions: Lock, Flanker

Representative team: Ireland

Clubs: Barnhall, Bective Rangers, St Mary's College RFC, Leinster, Toulouse

Nicknames: the Barnhall Bruiser, the Milkman, the Horsebox

OF ALL THE opponents that Trevor Brennan came up against in his career, it was the combination of Jeff Blackett, Rod McKenzie and Achille Reali that proved the toughest. Were these three a particularly robust back-row combo who relished facing off against Brennan's own brand of immense physicality? No. They weren't players. They were middle-aged men in suits. A judge and two solicitors, who in March 2007 made up the disciplinary committee of European Rugby Cup (ERC), the governing body and organiser of the Heineken Cup. Their verdict on Brennan was far harsher than any trash talk, team talk or newspaper columnist sniping he'd ever received.

It was the view of the Committee that Mr Brennan's behaviour was completely unjustified and that he caused serious harm to an innocent spectator and significant damage to the image of Rugby Union. The Committee could not envisage more serious Misconduct in relation to spectators and believed that the maximum permissible suspension was appropriate.

The Committee therefore imposed on Mr Brennan a lifetime suspension from playing Rugby Union and also imposed a lifetime ban on Mr Brennan from participating in any capacity in tournaments organised by ERC.[93]

The lifetime ban was subsequently reduced to five years on appeal, but it still meant that Trevor Brennan had played his last game of rugby.

So what led to the "serious harm" being inflicted upon the "innocent spectator"? Well, before we look at that incident, I think we need to go back to the very start, as the road to that fateful day gives plenty of clues.

Born in 1970 to a tightly knit working class family, Brennan grew up in Leixlip in Kildare, a town about 45 minutes' drive west of Dublin. His outstanding biography, *Heart and Soul*, written with *Irish Times* journalist Gerry Thornley, shares his childhood in rich detail: a mix of sports, rough and tumble with his brothers and a very strong work ethic. He was peeling potatoes in a local chip shop aged just 12 and worked as a barman and bouncer, among other jobs, through his teenage years. He saved enough money so that aged 18, he and his 16-year-old brother bought the rights to a milk round and, along with their dad, went into business together delivering to around 600 houses in the early hours.

Whilst Irish rugby has changed in recent years, it still draws many of its top players from a core group of fee-paying schools in the Dublin area, some in Cork and Limerick, and Protestant grammar schools in Northern Ireland. In the 2019 Irish Rugby World Cup squad, of the 23 players that received a post-primary education in the Republic of Ireland, 16 attended fee-paying institutions. The route from the big rugby schools into pathways and academies and club, provincial and International representation is well trodden.

Brennan, however, took a different road. While working full-time, he started playing for his local club, Barnhall, as a junior, then joined Bective Rangers in Dublin for his first taste of senior rugby. This was in 1992 – a time before professionalism, provincial rugby supremacy, the Heineken Cup and the Celtic League. The league pyramid he joined, the All-Ireland League (AIL), had only recently been inaugurated and Brennan took quickly to the higher standard, for the first time switching from No. 8 to blindside flanker.

Even as one of the younger and more inexperienced players on the team, he feared no opponent, not even fellow hard man Wayne Shelford (profiled earlier in the book), then in the twilight of his career. They met when he played for Northampton in a friendly against Bective and the New Zealander ended up "rolling around the pitch" with the 19-year-old Brennan.[94]

Brennan received the first red card of his career for fighting with Irish International Brian Rigney and had another dust-up with an ex-All Black, Mike Brewer, in a fixture against Blackrock – exchanging punches before being asked to leave the field, and continuing their spat all the way back into the changing rooms.

During his formative years playing senior rugby, he was being noticed for his talent and physicality, but also his temperament. Brennan said, "It seemed as if my 'incidents' were now being highlighted a bit more. I didn't care really – maybe it was because my adversaries were usually high profile... I suppose I did have a bit of a reputation as a hard man and a firebrand. Growing up, I had been in fights, I had been beaten up, I'd given out a few myself... I'd always had an aggressive streak. Yes, I still reckon my 'rep' is a bit of a myth. Sometimes one incident can be highlighted then it's 'give a dog a bad name'.

"I don't think I was in any more rows than some others. These were hard men, and at that time there were more hard men around. That's the way the game was."[95]

His career was to take him next to St Mary's College RFC, one of Dublin's leading clubs, where he captained the team to a league triumph in 2000, and he was soon turning out as a regular for Leinster, which during Brennan's period in Dublin had moved from being a purely representative team playing relatively infrequently in the Interprovincial Championship and occasionally against visiting teams, into the slick, professional outfit we see today.

Brennan was a big personality, and always quick with a laugh and a story. Plenty of his Leinster teammates have anecdotes about him in their autobiographies, but Girvan Dempsey in particular loved playing with the big man from Kildare. "Trevor is one of the great rugby characters... and is responsible for my funniest moment in rugby. It was one of my first starts for Leinster and we were playing Treviso on a preseason tour of Italy. After we flew into the airport and collected our bags, our manager at the time, Jim Glennon, came in to tell us there would be a delay because there was a difficulty with Dean Oswald's passport and the problem was being compounded by the language barrier. Trevor immediately piped up, 'I'll sort it for you, I know the lingo.'

"We were all stunned because Trevor was not known for his linguistic skills. When we turned to him and asked him when he had learned to speak Italian, he coolly replied, 'I worked in Luigi's chip shop one summer.'"[96]

The jokes would flow at Leinster, but Brennan took the step-up in playing standards in his stride, and soon Ireland came calling. He made his International debut on the 1998 tour of South Africa, which he calls the pinnacle of his career. Brennan might now have been representing his country, but he still applied his unique approach to the game, whoever the opposition were.

In his second Test, a 33-0 defeat to South Africa, he got firmly involved in the constant scraps throughout the game, describing it as both "like a battlefield from an old war movie" and "right up my alley".[97]

In truth, Brennan's Ireland career never fully took off and his 13 caps won across three years were not a fair representation of his talent and ability. A mixture of injuries and fierce competition with the likes of Eric Miller, allied with the doubts that some had about his temperament and his ultra-honest post-match interviews, meant he never truly established himself in the squad.

He did play in the 1999 World Cup, and it is probably the events of the game against Australia for which he is best known in an emerald green jersey. The fists were once again flying but this time he was more sinned against than sinner.

Wales were the official hosts of this tournament, but the games were sprinkled around the Home Nations, with Ireland facing off against Australia at the old Lansdowne Road. From a restart Brennan clipped Jeremy Paul with his elbow, but he is adamant it was an accident: "He was alright. If I was going to do it deliberately, I'd have done it right."[98]

Paul was tackled and in the ensuing melee, Brennan and opposition No. 8 Toutai Kefu faced off against each other. They exchanged a few punches, and then both Brennan's arms were held back by two of Kefu's teammates, while a bandage that had been applied earlier in game was pulled down over his eyes. He couldn't move or see, and received about ten punches straight to the head from Kefu. All this was happening in the Australian 22 after a long clearance kick; only one Ireland teammate, Andy Ward, came to help as most of the team were facing the other way, jogging up to a line-out.

After a brief consultation between the referee and the touch judges, Australia were awarded a penalty, and a bloodied and dazed Brennan was substituted a few minutes later. Australia went on to win the match 26-3, and a cowardly Kefu avoided attending the post-match reception, keeping away from an angry Brennan.

Both men were cited, and, not for the last time, a trio of middle-aged suits held Brennan's fate in their hands. Although they acknowledged that Brennan had been held back and punched, as he had raised his hands first, he received a 10-day ban, and Kefu just four additional days away from playing with 14. But the way the fixtures lay, they both missed two matches – their final group games, then in Brennan's case the quarter-final play-off defeat to Argentina, and for Kefu a quarter-final win over Wales. The defeat to Argentina was by four points, and Ireland had at one point held a 12-point lead, so it's no stretch of the imagination to think that Brennan's presence may have seen Ireland win that game. But they didn't and that was end of the World Cup for the Irish, while Kefu and Australia went on to win it.

After the World Cup disappointment, Brennan returned to his club rugby but drifted out of the picture for national team selection and, at 28, was no longer always starting for Leinster. Instead, he was increasingly viewed as a highly effective impact substitute. He began to look elsewhere for opportunities, and whilst clubs in England and Wales were interested, it was an unexpected call from French giants Toulouse that re-energised his career. One of their scouts had been impressed by his Celtic League performances and in came the offer. He went from earning €3,000 a month at Leinster to €10,000 at Toulouse, plus a hefty bonus.

A player whose career could easily have begun to wind down was now joining the biggest team in France – and arguably Europe – and lining up alongside the likes of Vincent Clerc, Frédéric Michalak and Émile Ntamack under the watchful eye of French coaching legend Guy Novès.

It may have been a new country but Brennan still had the same attitude to the game. Here he is talking about his Toulouse debut: "I was gently eased in as a second-half replacement.

Bodies piled on top of me as my head was left sticking out the side of a ruck. Then I was hit by two haymakers. This was my first match in France. A friendly. Welcome to France. By the time the ruck broke up, there was blood gushing everywhere... I went berserk looking for the guy who clobbered me, even pushing the referee out the way. I had to have 12 stitches."[99]

There were certainly plenty of tussles in his games for Toulouse, but the fans took straight away to this heart-on-his-sleeve, hard-tackling Irishman, and his performances were superb. Just six months into a two-year contract, he was offered a two-year extension. His wife and two young sons were with him and he quickly learned the language and assimilated into life in south-west France.

More was to come. Whilst Lansdowne Road was never the happiest of hunting grounds for Brennan in an Ireland shirt, he would make his mark there in the final of the 2003 Heineken Cup. The only non-Frenchman in the starting XV, he delivered a huge performance as Toulouse beat Perpignan 22-17 to lift the trophy. The celebrations, combining busloads of his family and friends from Leixlip and Barnhall with his French teammates, also equated to some serious action post-match and the cup ended up in Brennan's bed.

Two years later and another Heineken Cup would be secured with an 18-12 win over Stade Français, and Brennan again started the match. In between these triumphs, he had featured in another final: a narrow loss to Wasps. Three finals in three years is truly remarkable and a credit to his levels of consistent performance at this highest level of rugby.

However, this glorious run came to a shuddering and abrupt halt on Sunday 21 January 2007 in a Heineken Cup group game against Ulster. Brennan was on the substitutes' bench and, not long after half-time, was told to warm up behind the posts. In the first half there had been a "bit of banter" from the Ulster fans as he and his teammates warmed up, but in the second half he was alone, and it was different.

"There was more banter, but maybe because I was on my own, I took more exception to it than I ought to. I said to the supporters, 'Steady on, lads.' And then I thought I heard something that simply turned a switch on in my head. I jumped over the wall and went for a supporter in what was without doubt the most reckless and stupid act I have ever committed."[100]

The cameras of Canal+ didn't capture the moment, but photographers did and they are stark images. The Ulster fan that Brennan hit, a 25-year-old solicitor from Belfast based in London called Patrick Bamford, was not pitchside but around six rows up and took several punches to the face before Brennan relented.

The Santa Claus hat he was wearing offered little protection to the barrage that fell upon him.

What was (or wasn't) said has never been proved and probably never will be.

In the days following, French newspaper *L'Équipe* had Brennan stating he'd heard the Ulster fans singing a song calling his mother a whore. And that one (presumably Bamford) looked him in the eyes and repeated it, which made him wade into the crowd.[101]

George Brennan, Trevor's uncle, called in to the popular Irish phone-in radio show *Liveline* to state that in addition to the slurs on his mother, there was a sectarian element to what the Ulster fans said, with one calling Brennan a "Fenian bastard". Trevor Brennan has never made this claim.

The Ulster fans have a different viewpoint. Julian Fowler, a Northern Irish BBC reporter who was attending the match as fan, wrote on the BBC website, "A number of the Ulster supporters started to chant, 'Your pub's a load of rubbish'. 'Rubbish' wasn't exactly the word they used, but it wasn't that much more offensive than that. He [Brennan] turned towards the crowd and climbed over a barrier and walked up the steps towards the eighth row where this fan was sitting. There was a sustained, repeated attack and I saw at least half a dozen, if not more, punches."[102]

Bamford flew home to London on the night of the incident and spent the following day in his local Accident and Emergency department – the right side of his jaw was badly swollen but his injuries weren't more serious. He has always protested that he was innocent of serious slurs, stating, "I cannot accept that any circumstances can justify his violence," and in 2008 he received libel damages from *The Irish Star* and *The Sun* over their reporting of the incident. The previous year, he had successfully sued *The Guardian* newspaper.[103]

An ignominious incident, whichever way you look at it. Brennan was fined €25,000 and whilst the lifetime ban was downgraded to five years, his playing career was over.

"I know better than anyone what I did was wrong. But a life ban? What was their point? Did they want my punishment to be a deterrent? No player is likely to ever repeat what I did. And if one did, in the heat of the moment, he'd hardly start mentally flicking through the history of cases such as mine before making a clinical decision to jump a wall and go after a spectator," Brennan said.[104]

The incident went around the world, comparisons being made with Eric Cantona's 1995 kung-fu kick into the crowd at Crystal Palace (which resulted in only a nine-month suspension) and a host of petitions were signed urging an easing of the ban, including one organised by the Provale, the French players' union, and signed by every professional club in France.

But that was that: the playing days of Trevor Brennan were gone, ended by a moment of red mist. In his book he admits that his wife Paula, usually the calmer of the pair, on being told the news, went "ballistic" at the timing of his sudden unemployment, given that she was eight-and-a-half months pregnant at the time.

It's actually perhaps Zinedine Zidane's headbutt onto the chest of Marco Materazzi in the final of the 2010 World Cup that is more comparable to Brennan than the actions of Eric Cantona. Plenty of pop psychologists have provided their analysis of the incident, seeing it as the result of a lifetime of frustration – the stray comment hanging in the air being the straw that broke the camel's back. But I guess we will never really know.

Perhaps Brennan doesn't even really know.

Yet, despite this ban, his reputation in Toulouse remained intact – perhaps, dare I say it, was even enhanced by the incident. Rugby fans in this part of France are fanatical, and saw in Brennan the same level of passion and commitment that they display on the terraces every week. He was very much viewed as 'one of us' and this action, in its rawness and emotion, was perhaps one that many of them could understand.

But let's not just think Brennan was all brawn and no brain. In the five years he was at Toulouse he played in nearly every key game, including every semi-final and final. You don't get to this level of game time for the leading club in Europe just as a reward for being a fans' favourite.

What happened after the ban has only reinforced his affinity with Toulouse. He didn't move home to Ireland after his playing career was ended; instead he runs a bar-brasserie in his new home village of Castelginest called Brennan's, and another smaller bar, Brennan's Snug, nearby. He and his wife Paula have become dual nationals, and there's more. All three of their sons play rugby and the two eldest have already been capped Internationally at youth level. Not, however, for Ireland, but for France. Danny Brennan won the U20 World Cup in 2018 – for a treat, search 'Daniel Brennan's hilarious reaction to beating New Zealand' on YouTube to hear his still broad Irish accent, despite proudly wearing the French shirt. His 6' 5" brother Josh has, in 2020, been called up for the French U20 squad, and looks set to be a big player in more ways than one.

So the Brennan rugby story looks set to have some new chapters coming soon.

The story of the blue-collar lad working his way from delivering milk and playing rugby for fun in Kildare, to being a leader of French rugby aristocrats is a special one, with the final jarring moment of sudden violence that ended it making the story all the more unique.

You wouldn't want to face Brennan on the pitch, but you'd certainly want him on your team.

The man who Brennan respects most was his coach at Toulouse, Guy Novès, so perhaps we should give him the final word. "I rediscovered in Trevor's game the behaviour of those amateur players giving their all for their jersey, their colleagues and their club."[105]

WADE DOOLEY

"The poor guy had flipped completely. In fact,
I'm sure I've picked up saner people at work
and thrown them into the back of a police van."

FACTFILE

Full name: Wade Anthony Dooley
Born: 2 October 1957, Warrington, England
Position: Lock
Representative teams: Lancashire, North of England, British Police, England, British & Irish Lions
Clubs: Preston Grasshoppers, Fylde, New Brighton
Nicknames: the Blackpool Tower, the Big Dipper

THERE'S BEEN A long and rich connection between members of the police force and rugby union. A steady stream of the boys in blue graced International pitches, and whilst professionalism means they are no longer supplying players at the top level, the legacy lives on with current Wales head coach Wayne Pivac being a former New Zealand detective, as is World Cup-winning coach Steve Hansen.

When it comes to the more social parts of rugby, and in particular some of the rowdier aspects of touring, there are several stories of police involvement of a different nature. A whole chapter could be filled with high jinks on 1970s Lions tours, but the 1974 South African expedition was particularly lively. One night in Port Elizabeth, after a lot of drinking, the more boisterous members of the squad took to trashing some of the hotel rooms. It remains unclear if the Lions or The Who were the first to begin this particular trend. As furniture splintered, water from the sinks overflowed and fire extinguishers were sprayed, an angry hotel manager sought out their captain, Willie John McBride. He was not part of the wrecking crew – instead, he was sitting cross-legged on his bed in his pants and smoking his pipe.

"Mr McBride," the manager screamed, "your players are wrecking my hotel." The farmer from Ballymena looked up, took a puff on his pipe, and enquired, "Are there many dead?"

"I've called the police," the manager replied. "And tell me, these police of yours," McBride said, "will there be many of them?"

Fast forward 15 years and there would be several policemen already in the Lions hotel, with Paul Ackford, Dean Richards and Wade Dooley trading blue for red on the Lions' successful tour of Australia. Ackford, an Inspector in London's Metropolitan Police, came in at 6' 4" and Richards, a constable in Leicestershire, was 6' 3", but towering over them was Dooley at 6' 8".

Dooley was born to be big. Pity his mother Edith when her bonny boy was born, weighing 10lb 10oz. In the 1950s the average birth weight was 7lb 3oz and it is recalled in his autobiography that the midwives paraded him round the ward to show the fellow maternity patients. Let's hope they'd already had their babies by the time they saw baby Dooley!

With his size also came a strong police heritage: his father (himself 6' 5") and great-grandfather were both officers of the law. His great-aunt Amy was also in the force, and being over 6' had her own reputation for being able to sort out pub fights without calling for backup from her male colleagues.

So it was no surprise that on leaving school he went into the police force in Blackpool. Despite the Lancashire resort being a lively beat, Dooley maintains that he rarely got involved in physical confrontation. He recalls in his entertaining (and wittily named) biography, *The Tower and the Glory: The Wade Dooley Story*, his own way of dealing with a physical threat: "When it comes to dealing with violent situations as a policeman, I have always adopted the 'softly, softly' approach my father taught me. The most important concept is never to rush in, just walk calmly up to the problem and more often than not the situation resolves itself."[106]

Him being 7'2" in his helmet no doubt helped!

Dooley was remarkable in playing 55 times for his country and going on two Lions tours but playing all his club rugby outside the top flight, for Preston Grasshoppers in the fourth division of the English pyramid. He didn't get his first England cap until the relatively late age of 27, but crucially in preparing him for the International game, alongside his club games he was still playing at a higher level in representative rugby for Lancashire, the North and the British Police.

When he was first selected for England, he was virtually unknown – but not to the then England coach, Dick Greenwood, who as a Lancastrian knew all about him through the county set-up. Once he'd made his debut, against Romania, Dooley became a fixture in the England team until 1993 and was part of a playing core that grew together, taking the red rose from Five Nations also-rans to World Cup finalists.

Whilst he may have adopted a 'softly, softly' attitude to policing, he took a more robust approach to rugby. In 1987 he achieved infamy for his role in that year's Five Nations fixture between Wales and England, better known as the 'Battle of Cardiff'. Neither team was of a particularly strong vintage in this era, but Wales were just about keeping ahead of their old rivals. England came into the game on the back of defeats to Ireland and France, and they were determined not to be cowed in Cardiff.

In just the second minute, England's Steve Bainbridge and Wales' Steve Sutton (also a policeman) tussled and spat angry words at each other in a line-out. They were pacified, but a minute later all hell broke loose as the forwards piled into a brawl and elbows and punches were thrown around.

Suddenly Welsh lock Phil Davies (yes, also a policeman), following a punch from Dooley, staggered out of the melee and collapsed, crumpling to the floor. Bill McLaren, incredulous at the scenes so early in the game, said on the commentary, "I tell you, this has got to be sorted out – what a start to an International. Phil Davies on the ground, punches thrown, two men completely on the deck."[107]

As the players were separated by officials, Davies tentatively stood up, blood streaming down his face and his eye already swelling up.

Graham Dawe, recalling the match on its 30th anniversary, said, "He was just in the wrong place at the wrong time. Somebody obviously upset Wade – Wade Dooley would sometimes hit his own teammates in training. I think Wade Dooley just thought, 'just crack on'."[108]

Dooley recalls a particularly aggressive pre-match, with English players spat on by Welsh fans and the captain Richard Hill "so psyched up he was virtually bouncing off the walls", ahead of a "lively, to say the least" team talk.

And then the game started, and almost immediately degenerated into a huge fight. Dooley recollects the incident. "All hell broke out around me but I just followed the play, only to see a Welsh fist flash at Jon Hall as he drove through onto the ball. I saw red, literally. It was a gut reaction, totally spontaneous. I lashed out at Hall's assailant, completely unaware of his identity, and the punch landed with a sickening thud on the side of Davies' face."[109]

Dooley escaped censure on the pitch (there were no video replays in those days, remember) but Phil Davies was forced to leave the field, injured. Dooley and Davies had played together for the Police and considered each other friends. Wales would go on to win the game 19-12, but there would be repercussions for Dooley. Some in the media called for criminal proceedings and several TV camera crews were following him when he was back on the beat in Blackpool on Monday morning.

No additional punishments followed, but he was dropped for England's next game as a disciplinary measure, as were fellow England forwards Gareth Chilcott and Graham Dawe, along with Richard Hill, who as captain on the day was held responsible for the team's ill-behaved performance by the Twickenham top brass.

Davies didn't want to take things further. Dooley had called his house in the days following the match: "Phil's mother answered the call, as he was out at the time. From her reaction you would have thought she was talking to her long-lost son... A warm-hearted lady who assured me there was nothing to worry about and promised to get Phil to ring me back. Sure enough, he did, and the message was simple: 'Forget it. It's over and done with.'"[110]

Whilst his England career suffered a brief blip after his tussle with PC Davies, the incident didn't hold him back. When Paul Ackford joined the team, the two formed a formidable second-row partnership, and Dooley was selected for the Lions tour to Australia in 1989. There he overtook Welsh rival Bob Norster to secure starts in the second and third Tests of the successful series.

The Lions tourists were no shrinking violets when it came to the physical aspects of the game, as Mike Teague – a tough customer himself – recalls. "What the Australians expected from northern hemisphere sides was for them to turn the other cheek – 'soft Pommies' was the phrase I recall. However, we had some pretty handy guys on the tour like Dean Richards, Wade Dooley, David Sole and Finlay Calder. We were in our late 20s, the right age, and come to the height of our powers. We were battle hardened 'circuit boys' who had been around."[111]

Building on the Lions' success, Dooley played in the 1991 World Cup, where England narrowly lost out to Australia in the Twickenham final, and he starred in the England team which secured successive Grand Slams in 1991 and 1992. Dooley's hard-man credentials were put to the test most during this period in a series of brutal matches against the French. The Five Nations fixture between the two in 1991 was a real battle, but appeared like a stroll in the park compared to what happened the following year.

Effectively a Five Nations title decider, both camps vowed pre-match that the game would not descend into violence – but once the whistle went, this was quickly forgotten. The two teams went at it, and just after half-time, with England comfortably leading, French discipline completely collapsed. An Olivier Roumat punch knocked Dooley briefly unconscious; on coming round, he turned to the referee, Stephen Hilditch, and – perhaps with an eye to dishing out his own punishment – begged him, "Ref, do not send that fucker off."

The violence would continue. Grégoire Lascubé (another policeman) who had hit Dooley in the ear so hard in the World Cup quarter-final the previous year that he had briefly deafened him, was sent off for repeatedly stamping on Martin Bayfield (yes, a policeman too)'s head and banned for six months. Minutes later the France hooker, Vincent Moscato, was sent off for – in the words of Dooley – "going berserk" at a scrum. "The poor guy had flipped completely. In fact, I'm sure I've picked up saner people at work and thrown them into the back of a police van."[112]

This was the first occasion in the Championship's entire history when two men were sent off in one game. England won 31-13 and would go on to claim the Grand Slam.

But this wasn't the only incident for Dooley in an otherwise successful season. In a 25-9 win at Murrayfield, he had a running battle with a young Doddie Weir, who was on the receiving end of a Dooley elbow and suffered a perforated eardrum.

"It was not a premeditated attack, purely a spur-of-the-moment reaction, and really just the next instalment in our ongoing battle... Doddie had been intent on winding me up, and he had succeeded."[113]

Whilst he received no official sanction, and he and Weir shared a beer post-match, the media again focused on the incident, particularly with this moment of red mist being juxtaposed against his profession. His erstwhile Lions colleague, the Scot John Jeffrey, publicly stated that he wanted him banned for life.

But he played on, and following on from his key role in two Grand Slams, Dooley was selected for his second Lions tour, the 1993 trip to New Zealand. He would almost certainly have played in the Test series, but sadly the sudden death of his father would end his tour. He returned home for the funeral and after a period of mourning was unfortunately not allowed to rejoin the touring party. A replacement, Martin Johnson (profiled later in the book), had already been called up and as a result the antiquated, inflexible 'tour agreement' forbade Dooley's return. This was the last truly amateur Lions tour and this administrative inflexibility only further highlighted the need for rugby to move towards a more professional approach.

The treatment of the popular Dooley upset the squad, as Will Carling recalled: "We had all known Wade Dooley's dad. It was a chance for this great amateur game to show the world what a great amateur game it is. If rugby had been a professional game, I might have understood – it would have cost a lot of money to have paid the extra man. But this was a player who had won 50-plus caps for his country, whose father loved rugby and would have wanted him to come out... Even now I can't believe the Home Unions behaved like that."[114]

After the Lions tour, Dooley retired from England duty to continue as a police officer, serving until 2007. Upon retirement from the force, and in an exquisite case of a poacher-turned-gamekeeper, Dooley took up a role as a Rugby Football Union citing officer for the Guinness Premiership and newly formed Championship.

"I suppose it's an extension of what I have been doing for the past 30 years – in effect it's policing rugby," said Dooley at the time of his appointment. "As a player I never minded the rough and tumble of the game, but it needs to be a clean contest. Now with all the camera angles, players are going to be spotted if they commit any foul play; there is no hiding place."[115]

News of his appointment must have brought a wry smile to many of his former opponents. They might have been equally surprised at what he also did next – running, alongside his wife Sharon (a former police officer too), the Dizzy Ducks Tea Rooms in the village of Wrea Green, near Preston. Among a flurry of great reviews on TripAdvisor, the size of the portions is a recurrent theme: "The cakes have to be seen to be believed – to call the portions generous is an understatement," said one. I think it's likely Dooley was overseeing this aspect himself!

In running through Dooley's career, it is perhaps a little too easy to hop from one disciplinary issue to another. But he was rarely outdone in the line-out, was a better scrummager than many gave him credit for and scored some handy tries as well. When he started his International career, England were a pretty mediocre outfit, but he gave them a strong backbone that would help them achieve Five Nations success and a World Cup final, as well as see him gracing two Lions tours. He certainly made the most of his size, which was almost freakishly tall in the amateur days, but is now pretty average for International locks.

We can leave the final word on Dooley to a man who knows him well: Dudley Wood, the secretary of the RFU during his playing days. "Wade has done a couple of things that he and we regret and he has paid the price. They are history. Otherwise, he has had a wonderful career and is a friendly, quiet and gentle man."[116]

BAKKIES BOTHA

"When I caught up with him ten metres away,
I made him understand that I hadn't liked it...
I hate injustice."

HANDWRITTEN ON TAPE stretched around arms and on some headguards, the message said simply 'Justice 4'. Worn by the Springbok team and management during the third Test between South Africa and the British & Irish Lions in July 2009, the global audience couldn't miss them. The message was clear to those watching.

The response from the authorities was strong.

"The playing arena is no place for protest," the three-man International Rugby Board (IRB) committee, which included former Australian captain John Eales, said in its ruling, adding that the wearing of the armbands "showed a serious lack of respect and consideration for their opponents".[117]

The South African Rugby Union (SARU) was found to have failed to make any attempt to prevent the protest. An unarguable point, when team coach Peter de Villiers had himself worn one of the bands around the arm of his blazer. The punishment included a fine of £10,000 for the SARU, a £1,000 fine for team captain John Smit and £200 for each of the other Springbok players that day.

The IRB added: "The Independent Committee was unanimous in its view that, had it not been for the legal technicalities... both the SARU and the Springbok players and management would have faced much more serious sanctions, including a more severe fine in the case of SARU and the suspension of the Springbok players and management from the Rugby World Cup 2011."

So what was the justice that was being sought so publicly and so riskily? In a country where politics and rugby are so often entwined, it would be easy to imagine it might have been related to something bigger than sport.

But no. It was rugby.

The DIY dissent was to protest a two-week ban given to Springbok second row Bakkies Botha (hence the number 4 on the armbands) for a hit on Lions prop Adam Jones. Botha's impact left the Welshman with a dislocated shoulder that ended his tour during the Springboks' 28-25 victory at Pretoria in the second Test.

What is perhaps most remarkable about this situation was not so much the demonstration and the fact that South Africa risked missing the 2011 World Cup to make it, but that it was to protest the innocence of the hardest South African player of his generation, a pantomime villain to many, who for once was actually not guilty of what he'd been accused of.

Having lost the first Test, the Lions were 16-8 up after 44 minutes when Simon Shaw was tackled in midfield, a ruck was formed and Jones went in to add his considerable heft to the situation. As he leant his body over the ball to protect it, Botha, almost at the horizontal but still on two feet, powered almost head first into Jones, sending him reeling. The Lions medical team were soon on the pitch and Jones would leave with them, not to return.

Following this brutal, mesmerising encounter, which saw the Springboks roar back to tame the Lions and put six players in the hospital, much of the press attention was on the actions of the Springbok team, and Botha in particular. He received a two-week ban for 'dangerous charging' and was ruled out of the third and final Test. An appeal against the ban was thrown out, and John Smit stated at the time not just that there was nothing wrong with Botha's challenge but that the ban set a dangerous precedent. "I hope it's just a case of Bakkies being victimised. If not, it could change this wonderful game... Rugby is about running into each other at a million miles an hour and tackling each other at a million miles an hour, stitching oneself up afterwards and sharing a beer. We don't see any wrongdoing in that challenge."[118]

Adam Jones agreed with this assessment as he recalled the incident in his excellent 2015 autobiography, *Bomb*. "I was bent over at a ruck, trying to seal the ball off, when he appeared from nowhere and smoked me. I knew immediately something was wrong. The pain was acute and excruciating. My shoulder was smashed out of its socket, and my right arm was locked outwards in a strange saluting position."

The prop continued, "Bakkies Botha had built his reputation on his no-holds-barred aggression. I just happened to be the wrong man in the wrong place. I didn't feel individually targeted... if anything, I felt like it was my fault because I was in the wrong position. Fair play to him, he caught me a peach."[119]

Whilst the son has accepted the hit as part of the game, his mother offered no such forgiveness.

"Wales trained against Toulon in 2014 before our trial match, and by that time he [Botha] had joined their travelling band of Galacticos. I saw my mother later that night and she asked if he'd had the gall to come and speak to me. I replied that he'd shaken my hand, asked how I was, and that we'd had a civilised chat. She was disgusted that I'd given him the time of day. Mothers never forget."[120]

In this instance, despite what Lions fans, the UK and Irish press and Adam Jones' mum might have thought, Botha's hit was very, very hard but fair. On other occasions during his career, it wasn't always quite as easy to justify his actions.

Born John Philip Botha, but known since childhood as 'Bakkies' after the Afrikaans slang for 'bow-legged' – something that he left behind as he grew – even in Springbok rugby's land of giants, at 6' 7" and 19st 7lbs, Botha towered over most of his teammates. He is one of the most decorated rugby players of all time. Part of the 2007 World Cup-winning team, to date he is the only player to have won a hat-trick of both Super Rugby and European Cup titles. Alongside his caps and medals, he has also been labelled a "disgrace to International rugby"[121] and a "thug",[122] among other less kind epithets.

There are few rugby fans without an opinion on Bakkies Botha, and having seen him play against Wales at the Millennium Stadium and regularly on television, I too had a view that he might be a difficult character to get along with. So when he agreed to speak to me for this book, I was mildly apprehensive as to how the discussion might go. I needn't have worried. On picking up the phone, he immediately asked about how my family were and how coronavirus was being dealt with in London, and what came through in our discussion was just how truly happy he was with his career and his place in life.

"I went out on my terms. When I retired in 2015, I was offered the chance to carry on playing, and I could have – I was offered an extra year at Toulon. But I was happy to stop. Lots of players don't get the opportunity to decide when they stop playing, so I was lucky. And for me, rugby was part of my life, not my life. So to come back to South Africa, my family, the farming, the butcher business and cut out the sport was what I wanted. I was blessed throughout my career, and so I was by how it ended."

We'll revisit later where Bakkies is now, but to rewind to the beginning of his career, it started with a year at the Falcons in Gauteng, before joining the Bulls in Pretoria, where he would spend a decade from 2001 onwards. Botha played for the South African U19, U23 and A sides before making his full debut against France in 2002, in a game where he received a yellow card for stamping.

Botha's international reputation for his confrontational style truly began to take shape in August 2003, in the fallout from a 29-9 defeat to Australia. Post-match, Wallabies hooker Brendan Cannon accused Botha of eye-gouging and biting him, displaying a mark on his shoulder as proof. Whilst the referee missed it and video evidence was inconclusive, Botha was cited and although found not guilty of gouging, he was given an eight-match ban for "deliberately attacking the face".

Eddie Jones, then Australia coach, was livid about the South Africans' actions during this game, which also saw Springbok prop Robbi Kempson suspended for four weeks for hitting Australian No. 8 Toutai Kefu with a late and high tackle that saw the Wallaby stretchered off the pitch and spending a night in hospital suffering from spinal concussion.

"It's a deliberate tactic from the Springboks and it puts a whole slur on the game. They talked about it during the week before the game. Why else would you talk about it? We're absolutely filthy about what they did. We need to expose them. They really need to have a good look at themselves, because that sort of rubbish should not go on," said Jones – though he would later put his ire aside enough to be assistant coach to the South Africa side, including Botha, which won the 2007 World Cup.[123]

Botha formed a formidable partnership – 'the combo' – with fellow lock Victor Matfield, and both men played the full 80 minutes of the 2007 World Cup Final as they defeated England in Paris. This pairing was probably the strongest second-row partnership of this era, and although the more cerebral Matfield often got more of the plaudits, Botha had the edge in the line-out and was also explosive in the loose with ball in hand, picking up seven International tries. They played together 63 times for the Springboks, with Botha saying, perhaps only partly in jest, that "sometimes I feel we know each other better than we know our wives".[124]

Winning rugby's biggest prize didn't do anything to dampen Botha's fire. In April 2009 he received a three-match ban for striking Australian flanker Phil Waugh in a Super 14 match between the Bulls and the Waratahs. Later that year the incident with Adam Jones of the Lions would also take place. The following year, two of the most infamous incidents of Botha's career occurred.

In May 2010, 24 seconds into his first game as captain of the Bulls, against fellow South Africa Super 14 team the Stormers, he smashed head first into Gio 'the Pocket Dynamo' Aplon at a ruck, conceding a penalty at the time and then picking up a four-week suspension following a post-match review. His charge into the ruck was deemed to be illegal and similar to the Adam Jones citation in that "he dangerously and recklessly entered a ruck without using his arms or grasping onto a player". Botha would miss the play-offs and the final, but it didn't stop the Bulls winning their second consecutive title and their third in four years.

Two months later, 29 seconds into the South Africa v. New Zealand Tri Nations fixture, Botha would strike again, and this time there would be even more severe consequences. There is a huge rivalry between the two rugby superpowers, with the Springboks being the only nation that consistently beats the All Blacks. There is always an edge to this fixture, and on this particular occasion it exploded before even a minute of action had taken place.

Just inside South African territory, Kiwi scrum half Jimmy Cowan had a box kick charged down by Botha and both men turned to run after the ball. Cowan pulled back Botha's shirt and then outsprinted him. The Springbok waved his arms in protest, but his claims for a penalty were ignored. They both continued to chase the ball. The All Black won the foot race, neatly recovered the ball and spun it out to a teammate. Having passed the ball, Cowan fell onto the turf. Botha, just behind him, fell too and, as he was landing, his head connected with the scrum half hard in the back of the head.

The referee, despite being only a few metres away, missed it and failed to notice the big red lump on Botha's forehead that angrily emerged in the following minutes. But the collision was replayed multiple times both on television and in the stadium, to howls of outrage from the New Zealand fans and some disbelief from commentators. Botha received no immediate sanction for what he did to Cowan. His punishment would follow post-match – a nine-week ban that ruled him out of the entire Tri Nations. A Botha-less Springboks would finish bottom of the table, with just one win in six games.

The New Zealand coach that day, Graham Henry, thought the ban was light: "He's got a history. He's probably lucky he didn't get more than nine weeks."[125]

On being quizzed about his teammate's actions that day, Botha's captain John Smit offered a view that may not have been that helpful to his cause: "I don't approve of any of my players playing outside the rules and it was an ill-disciplined, very poor first half, which meant we had no momentum. Only Bakkies can explain what goes on in his head."[126]

Botha expressed considerable remorse at the time: "I sincerely regret the incident. I have let my team, my country and family down and I have done an injustice to the Springbok jersey and what it stands for."

He continued, "I apologise to Jimmy Cowan and the New Zealand rugby public for what happened. Rugby is a physical sport but it has to be played within the boundaries and spirit of the law. I truly regret my actions and will make sure that I put the extended time away from the game to positive use and return to playing with the right attitude."[127]

But speaking to French newspaper *Midi Olympique* in 2020, it was a different story from the big South African when asked if he regretted the incident with Cowan. "No, not a single second. And if I were to relive this situation, I would do the exact same thing," he said.

"That day in Auckland I was battling with Cowan following a kick. I was faster than him. I had passed him and he pulled me by the shirt to slow me down. When I caught up with him ten metres away, I made him understand that I hadn't liked it... I hate injustice."

Botha concluded, "It's not something I'm proud of. I kind of dropped the Springboks that day. And Jimmy Cowan won the mini-battle. But I would react in exactly the same way today... it's still the fault of the No. 9. They talk too much and know better than anyone how to get you out of the game."[128]

Speaking to me for this book, Botha admits that he reacted stupidly against Cowan. "He did pull me back, but I lost it that day and shouldn't have."

He continues by explaining that the rivalry with the All Blacks was always very keen. "They were always the hardest opponents we faced and there was no better player than Richie McCaw that I came up against. My role was clear when playing against them: make the breakdown brutal. If McCaw or any of the New Zealand boys had to take a moment to look out for me, then I knew I was winning. When I played them, I always wanted them to know I was coming for them, and the biggest compliment I ever received was from [South Africa manager] Jake White, who said he could see they had fear in their eyes during the game."

The Cowan incident solidified his reputation as the bogeyman of rugby but, after serving his ban, he would go on to win a further 17 caps for his country, and appear at the 2011 World Cup, though his tournament was cut short after an injury against Namibia in the pool stages. In total he made 85 appearances for the Springboks across 12 years.

In 2011, having won the top prize in southern-hemisphere rugby three times, he headed north to take his particular brand of rugby to Toulon in France. The team he had joined was a remarkable one, funded by the wealth of comic book tycoon Mourad Boudjellal and as close to a 'Galacticos' approach to rugby as we are likely to see. Botha would play alongside the likes of England's Jonny Wilkinson, Australia's Matt Giteau, New Zealand's Carl Hayman, Wales' Gethin Jenkins as well as fellow Springboks Juan Smith and Bryan Habana, to name but a few of his illustrious teammates.

Botha played some of the best rugby of his career in France, and it wasn't just his all-star teammates that would bring the best out of him – he loved the style of the game too.

Botha spoke passionately about his time in France: "I had an amazing time there. Some people thought I was just going there to draw a pension, but no, I had to perform every time I played and I was there to win cups, which we did. French rugby has a slower tempo than Super Rugby but is far more physical. I've never been known for my pace, so that worked well for me. I remember my first game there. Bang! I was straight into it. And to be in a team with all the great players that they had there was a real privilege. I can't see that kind of squad ever being built again. Probably my only regret in my career was not going to France earlier. I could have gone in 2007 but my loyalty to South Africa kept me there."

He also added that the referees were "pretty relaxed" in France, which may have supported his success. Botha's four years in France saw him receive only two yellow cards. That's not to say he wasn't at times a controversial figure during his spell on the French Riviera. In a Heineken Cup quarter-final win over Leicester in 2013, on a bullocking run towards the try line, Botha charged straight through Marcos Ayerza, who, in attempting to tackle him, broke his collarbone in two places.

Botha wasn't punished either during the game or afterwards, and Leicester Director of Rugby Richard Cockerill, a man not unfamiliar with disciplinary boards from his own playing days, criticised the authorities for this, feeling Botha should have been cited for an 'excessive use of the knee' during the charge.

"Marcos has broken his collarbone in two places. He will have surgery to have it plated and repaired, and he will be out for three months," explained an incensed Cockerill. "I am pretty sure it is against the laws of the game to hurdle into a player – and that has caused damage to our player, who will now miss the rest of the season."[129]

But Cockerill's complaints went unheeded. Botha's hit on Ayerza can also be filed under very, very hard but fair. Botha retired in 2015, aged 36, his last game being the Heineken Cup Final, where he helped Toulon beat French rivals Clermont. It was a final success in a remarkable career which saw him win three Super Rugby titles, three European Cups, three Currie Cups, a Top 14 Championship, two Tri Nations titles plus the Lions series win in 2009 and, of course, a World Cup in 2007.

On retiring from playing, Botha, a family man and committed Christian, returned to South Africa to farm in the Limpopo region of Northern Transvaal and run Bakkies the Butcher, selling organic meat from his farm, as well as his own spices, herbs, seasonings, sauces and condiments. Check him out on Facebook!

Reviewing his career by writing this profile, the comments posted below the myriad YouTube videos of his greatest hits and online articles about him show what a divisive figure Botha is. For every quote stating he's a legend, there's another saying he's a thug and a liability. And this split isn't necessarily by country – there's some negative opinion in South Africa as well as positive viewpoints among the supporters of those countries he terrorised.

On retiring, he acknowledged that the greater scrutiny of the game and the emergence of the television match official has shifted the sport away from players like him. "The game is different today. I loved the physicality of it but nowadays, the breakdown is a very different business. There's far more structure and coaching in the game today. But I always say, now they have data and science that can measure the mud under your fingernails, but they can't measure the size of your balls, and that is what is important on the pitch!"

Along with all the trophies and caps, there are several regrettable incidents in Botha's career, but his down-to-earth approach to the game, his clear love of the physical aspects of the sport and his openness about being no angel have made him a huge figure in modern rugby. Not just one of the hardest, but also one of the best players in our collection, Bakkies Botha is someone you would love to have alongside you when the going gets tough, but definitely not facing you as an opponent.

We'll let Botha have the final word as I ask him what, for him, really makes a hard man of rugby. "I was labelled 'the Enforcer' and that was truly an honour – I loved that role. For some guys the physical stuff doesn't come naturally but for me it does. I already mentioned McCaw, and Jerry Collins was certainly another player who deserved that title. We had some great battles. I played to the edge and sometimes, yes, I went over it. But you can't be seen to give an inch. And as I have to point out, I never received a red card – my punishments always came as post-match citings! Peter de Villiers, when he was Springbok coach, once told me that I was 'born to hurt people' and that for me was a huge compliment. I always played to see the fear in my opponents' eyes. But now? I am happy out in the country with my new life. Rugby was part of my journey, and I am blessed to learn what comes next."

TOMÁS LAVANINI

"He plays to the limit and sometimes he exceeds himself, but I want him by my side."

FACTFILE

Full name: Tomás E Lavanini

Born: 22 January 1993, Buenos Aires, Argentina

Position: Lock

Representative team: Argentina

Clubs: Hindú Club (Buenos Aires), Pampas XV, Racing Métro, Jaguares, Leicester Tigers

Nickname: *Lengua* (= the Tongue)

Lavanini admitted the act of foul play and accepted that it warranted a red card. He accepted that given his previous disciplinary record, he was not entitled to the full 50 per cent discount from the six-game entry point. Having considered all the evidence and after hearing from the player and his legal representative, the panel imposed a sanction of four matches.[130]

EVEN THE LATE Johnnie Cochran would have struggled to get Lavanini off the hook for this suspension, a result of a high tackle on England's Owen Farrell, and one that would end Lavanini's participation at the 2019 World Cup. In fact, he was lucky that two matches were shaved off at all.

It's fair to say, the boy has form.

Since winning his first cap in 2013, the 6' 7", 19+ stone second row has received five yellow cards and two reds in 56

International matches. In a particularly aggressive streak after the 2015 World Cup, he was carded four times in eight games.

Lavanini's card rap sheet includes dangerous charging, illegal clean-outs at rucks, kneeing opponents, deliberate knock-ons, and his favourite: no-arms tackles, which make up the majority of his offences. It's a remarkable record – remember, Bakkies Botha was not once sent off in his 85 International games – and one that as a young man, still playing, he has plenty of time to add to!

In 2017 he was red-carded in a home Rugby Championship fixture against South Africa after receiving two yellow cards. The first came after only nine minutes for a no-arms charge at Springbok prop Coenie Oosthuizen, then a deliberate, try-preventing knock-on just before the hour got Lavanini a second yellow card, followed by an automatic red.

It was a chaotic fixture which saw the visitors come away from Salta in the north of the country with a 41-23 win and, in addition to Lavanini's pair of cards, saw two further cards and two mass brawls.

He escaped further punishment when the organisers stated the sending off "was sufficient in itself and that no further sanction was appropriate".

It cleared him to play against world champions New Zealand when they came to visit Buenos Aires the following month. It was a 36-10 defeat for Argentina in which, after just 21 minutes, he'd receive a yellow card for a no-arms tackle. After this further breach of discipline, he didn't play again for his country for another year.

Lavanini in some ways lives up to the macho Latin stereotype, which becomes amplified when it comes to playing rugby, but that oversimplifies the history of the sport in his country.

Rugby was first played in Argentina by British expats in 1873 and quickly found a foothold as part of the curriculum in schools modelled on the traditions of UK private education. Argentina played its first International in 1910 against a visiting British team, with the wonderfully named Cornelius MacCarthy being their first ever try scorer. These early teams had a strong anglo-orientation, and the game long had a reputation for elitism, with the club game rooted in Old Boys of fee-paying or English-language schools.

A look at the jobs of some of the amateur-era Argentine greats does little to dispel this image: Hugo Porta was an architect, Felipe Contepomi a doctor, Diego Cuesta Silva a cardiologist and Pedro Sporleder a successful property developer. Perhaps it was the standard of education that made Argentina the last major nation to emerge from the amateur era. As recently as the 1999 World Cup, in which they reached the quarter-finals, only a handful of the squad were professional.

Professionalism has changed the game in every country and Argentina is no different, with their exploits at the World Cup in particular being a great aid in spreading rugby's popularity. A third place in 2007, another quarter-final in 2011 and a fourth place in 2015 have raised the sport's profile beyond its original narrow parameters. In 2012 they gained entry to the Tri Nations, turning it into the Rugby Championship. And whilst they have found wins against New Zealand, South Africa and Australia hard to come by, their club team the Jaguares (which included Lavanini from 2016–19) have been a success since starting to compete in Super Rugby in 2016, improving steadily and finishing as runners-up in 2019.

Argentina may have its own strong rugby pedigree but Tomás E Lavanini was born to a family of football rather than rugby fans.

"I was not a big fan of rugby as a boy. I only watched a few International games on television – I just got into it because some friends were. But once I started playing at Hindú [his first club], I began to enjoy it. Whist there, I was trained by great players such as Nicolás Fernández Miranda, his twin brother Juan Fernández Miranda, Lucas Ostiglia and others who played in the First Division. I also heard them talking about rugby at the bar and on hearing the stories, it gives you no choice but to be crazy about the game!"[131]

He made his debut for the Buenos Aires-based Hindú Club, one of the country's most successful teams, in 2012. Lavanini would then appear for the Pampas XV, perhaps one of the most unusual teams of the modern era. They were an Argentine team but based in South Africa and competing in their second-tier domestic competition, the Vodacom Cup, between 2010 and 2013, winning it once. Lavanini no doubt relished the hard-tackling South African rugby culture, and it clearly helped his career, as he would become an International and then join Racing Métro in Paris during this period.

He had represented the U20 team at the 2013 IRB Junior World Championship, and would make his full debut that year in a win over Uruguay. A few months later, he would make his first appearance in the Rugby Championship in a loss to South Africa and would be part of the squad at the 2015 World Cup.

As his career developed, so did his reputation for an extreme physicality, bordering on the reckless. He has become something of a YouTube rugby sensation, with a host of videos showcasing all his worst tackles to a variety of questionable backing tracks. The names of these compilations include 'Tomás Lavanini – Rugby's Biggest Thugs' and 'Is he the most reckless player in world rugby?' One created by an Argentinian fan takes a different view, and is named simply, 'Tributo'.

There's no doubt he does commit some awful tackles, and many of his cards seem to come for a no-arms clean-out of a ruck, coming in very low along the ground – almost at knee height – putting himself almost at as much risk as his opponent. Whilst tackling someone's knee is legal, it is not if you don't use your arms, or if they are at the back of the maul. This 'grasscutter' style of clear-out is a distinctive but dangerous trademark of Lavanini's.

Reviewing these videos, one particular action of his really stands out.

It came whilst playing for the Jaguares in February 2016, when he jumped and dropped his knee onto the Cheetahs' William Small-Smith as the centre was scoring a try. Lavanini got airborne just milliseconds before the ball was grounded and there was no attempt to disrupt its grounding – instead he just hit the poor, prone Small-Smith in the ribs with his knee. It's a cheap, painful shot against someone who couldn't defend himself. He was cited and suspended post-match.

Returning to Argentine colours in the June of that year, he did something nearly identical to France's Loann Goujon, kneeing the flanker in the head as he scored a try. A yellow card and suspension would follow.

I think it's fair to say that Lavanini could be described as a repeat offender.

His absences from the pitch have harmed his teams' chances of winning games, but his reputation has been factored into his playing ability and he has kept the backing of his International captain Agustin Creevy. Creevy told an Argentine journalist, "He plays to the limit and sometimes he exceeds himself, but I want him by my side. The day he doesn't have it, I don't know what I'm going to do."[132]

In May 2019, it was announced that after the World Cup of that year, Lavanini would be leaving the Jaguares and joining Leicester Tigers. The Midlands outfit were once built upon a formidable pack that included the likes of Martin Johnson, Graham Rowntree and Julian White, but the fear factor had long gone, with the 2018/19 season their worst for decades.

Tempting Lavanini back across the Atlantic was a way of attempting to regain this fearsome reputation. Whilst not directly acknowledging his discipline issues, Tigers head coach Geordan Murphy did give an indicator of what they were looking for in signing him: "Tomás has played an important part in a big, physical and impressive Pumas pack and he has a lot of experience for a player of his age. He brings a lot of the attributes we've been looking for in that area..."[133]

With anticipation building for Lavanini's arrival at Welford Road, Tigers fans would have enjoyed settling down to watch him face off against England in a World Cup group game. However, they only got to run their eye over their new addition for 18 minutes before he was sent off for the high tackle on Owen Farrell. To give Lavanini some credit, this was a less clear-cut card than many of his others and did foster some debate as to whether it was the correct decision.

The score at this point was only 5-3 to England, and Lavanini was clearly intent on putting in a huge hit on Farrell. Unfortunately, he got his angle wrong and ended up leading with his shoulder, which smashed into the Englishman's neck and jaw and forced him to jolt first backwards, then down onto the turf. Referee Nigel Owens' initial reaction was that it was not foul play, but on reviewing it on the video, saw it differently and sent Lavanini off. Deprived of the lynchpin of their pack, Argentina would end up losing 39-10. That was the end of Lavanini's World Cup, and his country would suffer a group-stage exit – the first time they have gone home so early since 2003.

Argentina coach Mario Ledesma said the red card was a fair call, and plenty of criticism came Lavanini's way. Mick Cleary of the *Telegraph* labelling him 'self-centred and negligent' was probably the pick of the barbs aimed at the big Argentinian.

So where does this leave Lavanini in our pantheon of hard men? After missing three games as part of his suspension for the hit on Farrell, he has quickly established himself as an impressive addition to the Leicester pack, but of course picked up two yellow cards in his first 13 games.

The way he plays, at times with a careless abandon for his own safety or that of those around him, is a bit of a throwback to a more brutal era. But between YouTube videos and clips shown on social media that build a reputation, and TMOs and citing commissioners keeping constant tabs on the on-field performance, it's near-impossible to get away with such misdemeanours at the top level. Plus there is now a growing emphasis on player safety and in particular on avoiding head injuries and concussions, so an extra focus is kept on anything above the shoulders. Factor all this together and it is difficult for a player to operate successfully at this level with an attitude like Lavanini's.

But he is only 27 and is still a fantastic player. He's very capable of wonderful takes in the line-out and solid ball handling, and (most of the time) is able to deliver hard but legal tackles. As his Instagram account shows, in May of 2020 he became a father for the first time, so perhaps his little son might be the balm he needs to welcome in a calmer second half of his career. Only time will tell.

JACQUES BURGER

"Everything hurts. It feels like you have been in a car accident. You tell yourself you won't be able to train the following day. Yet you always do. Rugby is a brutal game but I wouldn't change it for the world. I love it."

FACTFILE

Full name: Jacques Burger

Born: 29 July 1983, Windhoek, present-day Namibia

Positions: Flanker, No. 8

Representative team: Namibia

Clubs: Wildeklawer Griquas, Aurillac, Blue Bulls, Bulls, Saracens

Nicknames: the Widow Maker, Demolition Man

STAMPRIET IN CENTRAL Namibia isn't a place for those who don't like life to have some challenges. Once a colonial-era German trading post, this small, remote town is located within the Kalahari Desert and is entirely reliant on boreholes for its water. A hard place to farm needs a tough character – and few come flintier than Jacques Burger, who on retiring from playing for Saracens, eschewed the worlds of media work, business or coaching to fulfil his childhood dream and return to his native Namibia.

The 14,000-acre farm Burger now owns is covered by the distinctive red dunes of the Kalahari and crossed by the occasional lion or sheep-hungry crocodile. His closest neighbours are 15 miles away, so it's a different world from north London, which he, his wife and two young children used to call home when it was on the rugby pitches of Europe rather than the dusty plains of west Africa that Burger made his living.

Even in 2010, with years still to run on his playing career, his mind was already turning to tilling the soil back home. "I've wanted to do this since I was a kid and once I've stopped playing rugby, I'll do it for the rest of my days... Namibia is one big farm, although I don't come from a farming background myself. I was born in Windhoek [the capital of Namibia], which makes me a town boy. But I love the space and freedom of the outdoors, and this project will keep me busy when I retire from professional sport. Players all over the world struggle with life after rugby. I don't want to go through that, so I'm getting myself organised."[134]

And that's exactly what he has done since calling it a day for Saracens in 2016, after a highly successful five-season stay in the English Premiership. At just 32, you may have thought he still had some rugby left in him, but although this tough-as-teak player suffered and recovered from an astounding array of injuries, even his bionic body couldn't go on forever.

His injuries read like a training manual for a particularly demanding medical course, with an incomplete list featuring two broken cheekbones, nerve damage, keyhole surgery on the shoulder, broken and bruised ribs, torn quadriceps, high tibial osteotomy surgery – which realigns the knee joint – lateral kneecap release and four further keyhole surgeries on other parts of his body.

In the final two years of his career, Burger's injuries went into overdrive, and he told journalists when his retirement was already confirmed, "I've had six surgeries on my right knee, two on my right shoulder, two on my cheekbones and a broken hand. I've had all the screws and plates taken out now, but I carry them with me in my kit bag as a reminder."

He continued, "There are times when I worry about the future. I have two small kids and I would like to be actively involved in their lives. But when I play, I forget about safety and the future, which is probably why I'm in this situation. I would play for 50 more years if I could, but I can't."[135]

Burger's apparent lack of concern about physical safety was a thread running through his career, and one that has continued even into his retirement, sparking that most modern of furores – a Twitterstorm. In March 2019 he shared a video of a particularly brutal tackle in a South African schools' match between Monument and Paarl, alongside the explosion emoji. The tackle is legal, but crunchingly hard, and the weight mismatch between tackler and tackled results in an injury for the ball-carrier. Burger's tweet quickly received hundreds of replies, some applauding the tackle, others criticising the Namibian for cheering on this hit in an era when there is a growing focus on tackle safety and head injuries.

Burger responded to the criticism with some customarily direct advice for parents whose children play rugby: "Tell your kids there is a good chance of injuries if they play rugby. That's the reality. Work on better/safer techniques so they can be smarter, well-prepared rugby players. Also, don't forget to tell them to do their best and enjoy."

He would also later add, again on Twitter, "We should give our youngsters all the tools to be safe in rugby but we should never teach our kids to do things half-heartedly."

Anyone who has seen Burger on the pitch might find it hard to imagine this all-action forward not playing rugby, but his early days didn't mark him out as a future great. He was born in 1983 in Windhoek, in what was then South West Africa – the country only became officially known as Namibia in 1990 when it became fully independent of South Africa. There was no academy rugby or seamless transition through the ranks of a team. Instead, after leaving school, Burger sold photocopying paper and office supplies for two years, just playing at the weekends.

He didn't take his rugby too seriously, until he was called into a Namibian national squad by coach Danie Vermeulen in 2004. The chance to represent his country changed his life. "I wasn't in the mood to train, but I went along, in the worst shape of my life, and it was tough, proper old-school. For some reason I just kept going back and that period changed the journey of my life."[136]

Vermeulen would have offered additional inspiration, as he coached from his wheelchair. A powerful prop capped five times for Namibia, he was left paralysed in a car crash in 2000 aged just 24.

Burger made his debut at No. 8 for the Namibian national team in a 52-10 win over Zambia, the first of 36 caps. Newly inspired as an International, he headed to Kimberley in South Africa, where he signed for the Griquas, playing Currie Cup rugby before moving on to French club Aurillac in 2007, a year in which he also represented Namibia at the World Cup. Despite a positive performance in the first game – a 32-17 defeat to Ireland – the other group defeats, including an 87-10 loss to France, proved a chastening experience to a squad containing many amateurs.

After a season in the second tier of French rugby, he returned to Africa and the Currie Cup, where he joined the Blue Bulls. He played for the Pretoria outfit for one and a half seasons, but struggled to step up into Super Rugby, making just two appearances in that competition for the Bulls.

By 2010, his career was at a crossroads. He had an offer from Eddie Jones to join Suntory Sungoliath in Japan, but instead, it would be Saracens in north London where Burger would find his true club home. The club had recently been taken over by a South African consortium, who appointed Brendan Venter, a World Cup-winner in 1995 with the Springboks (a feat he accomplished whilst still practising as a doctor) as Director of Rugby in 2009. Venter quickly made changes, replacing 15 players in one tumultuous summer and looking to Africa to strengthen the squad. Venter had coached Burger for the African Leopards (a pan-African invitational team) in 2006, and when he got the chance to rebuild the Saracens team, the big Namibian was one of the first players he called.

Whilst not all the signings succeeded, a new era had truly dawned and Saracens, with Burger at the heart of their pack, would become the ascendant power in not just English but also European rugby. In his first season at the club, they would reach the Premiership final but fall just short against Leicester Tigers; the following year they would not be denied, turning the tables on the Tigers with a 22-18 win. Burger played the full 80 minutes in that second final, a tense game that had a riveting conclusion with the Tigers four points down, going through 32 phases before Saracens won a penalty, the match and their first ever league title in front of 80,000 fans at Twickenham. From being on the cusp of heading to the well-remunerated but relatively stress-free Japan, Burger was now playing in some of the biggest and most physically demanding games in world rugby.

Looking back on his career from retirement, he sees this as a very special time. "When I was with the Bulls, we won the Super Rugby title and the Currie Cup, but I wasn't really involved that much. At Saracens, I felt like a key player; that year [2010/11] I was nominated as Players' Player of the Year. It was an incredible season. We had massive belief – we knew that even if we were 20 points down, we could get back into a game. It wasn't arrogance, we just believed in the system, the coaches and everyone around us. We knew it was the right thing to do to be successful, and we were."[137]

At the 2011 World Cup, Burger captained the 'Welwitschias', as the Namibians are nicknamed, after the unusual plant native to their country. Although suffering four losses – including heavy reverses to South Africa and Wales, 87-0 and 81-7 respectively – Burger's reputation was enhanced. He was named as one of the top five players of the tournament, alongside Israel Dagg and Jerome Kaino of tournament-winners New Zealand, Wales' Jamie Roberts and Seán O'Brien of Ireland. His citation read:

> Consistently the shining light in his side, Namibia captain Jacques Burger demonstrated enough skill and fortitude to suggest he would legitimately earn a place in many of the higher-ranked teams at the tournament. Burger was a skipper who led by example. Even as opposition scores mounted, the 28 year old continued to tirelessly throw himself into the tackle and threaten turnover ball in the rucks. When it comes to judging Burger's contribution, the statistics tell the tale. The wholehearted flanker notched an impressive 64 tackles in Namibia's four matches.[138]

In being selected in this top five, he edged out the other opensides in the tournament – a list that included Richie McCaw, David Pocock, Sam Warburton and the equally physical Maurie Fa'asavalu of Samoa, while playing for a team that lost all their matches by an aggregate score of 266-44.

His heroics were all the more remarkable as he was carrying a knee injury going into that World Cup. He played four brutal games, then went straight back into the action for Saracens – but even for Burger it became apparent something was seriously wrong.

"Yes, I played on," he told *The Independent*. "But pretty soon I had to own up. I had to tell them: 'Look, I'm really sorry, but I can't carry on like this.'" It was then that he sought specialist advice, and discovered the true extent of the problem.

"I saw several specialists," he continued, "and what they saw was really worrying. There was so much bone damage in the knee, I was starting to go bow-legged. The operation was a major one: they call the procedure a high tibial osteotomy and, basically, it involved them changing the shape of my right leg and putting the kneecap in a different place to reduce impact and pressure in vulnerable areas. They told me my recovery would take at least a year. That was a tough thing to hear, and when I realised after a while that it would take a lot longer than that, it was tougher still."[139]

A long and intense period of physio and recuperation ensued, with some observers foolish enough to doubt they would ever see Burger on the pitch again, but after 14 months he was back for the start of the 2013/14 season. He had to look after his body a little bit more and the niggling injuries kept mounting up, but when on the pitch, his physicality and bravery remained untarnished.

"Every time I get back from my injuries, people ask whether I will change the way I play," he told *The Guardian*. "But I don't know any other way."[140]

In a crucial 16-9 Saracens win over rivals Exeter at Sandy Park, Burger made 36 tackles, at times almost single-handedly repulsing the Chiefs as they pummelled the visiting defence. Then, a few months later, despite carrying some further injuries, this Saracens team hit their peak in a stunning 46-6 win over Clermont in the Heineken Cup semi-final.

Although the final score might suggest a one-sided romp, that match was a real battle and Mick Cleary of *The Daily Telegraph* saw the heart of the victory in Burger's performance. "Burger's play was elemental: fierce, unrelenting, selfless and totemic. He broke Clermont's spirit, capturing the essence of this Saracens side by committing his body and soul to the cause. Where he went, sacrificing any notion of personal welfare as he hit hard, again and again and again, everyone else followed. He made 27 tackles, all of them ferocious, all of them influential, contributing to what was the most all-encompassing display from an English side in the 19-year history of European rugby."[141]

Charlie Morgan of *Rugby World* described the performance more poetically as Burger's *Mona Lisa*, while Burger himself gave some insight into the effort that went into it, stating sardonically, "Luckily I've got a face that hides pain well."

The following year, despite yet more injuries, he picked up another Premiership winners' medal with Saracens before heading to his third World Cup with Namibia. The Webb Ellis Cup looked like once again bringing the best out of the big man. After a spirited 58-14 defeat to eventual tournament winners New Zealand in the opening fixture, he scored two tries in a 35-21 defeat to Tonga in his nation's second match. Sadly, Burger's tournament, and indeed his International career, would be over just nine minutes into the next fixture against Georgia, when he suffered a concussion while bravely stopping their bulky centre Merab Sharikadze in full flow. Namibia would pick up their first ever World Cup point, a losing bonus point as they were edged out 17-16, but it is not hard to think they could have had so much more if their talismanic captain had been able to stay on the pitch.

He returned from the World Cup for one final season with Saracens before finally calling it a day in May 2016, and switching his attention to his farm back home in Namibia.

"To be honest, my body is going to be very happy to not be able to smash everybody every weekend, so the rest will do me really well," Burger told the Saracens website on his final weekend as a player. "I will honestly miss playing. There will be times when I'll wish I could play with the boys. There is no feeling like it, even when it is really tough and you're not really enjoying training because it's really hard, and you get stuck in to each other and you're part of that group," he continued.

Burger had a remarkable career, finding his calling at Saracens and becoming a true club legend in an era when the team was remarkably strong. The number of injuries he suffered during this period was astounding and few other players would have played on through them. With his shaggy hair and boxer's nose (broken too many times to count), once seen, few would forget him.

As one of the biggest tacklers in the game, his body does suffer the consequences. "A lot of times after a match you wake up in the middle of the night and you're like 'Oiyaya!' You can't get out of bed. Everything hurts. It feels like you have been in a car accident. You tell yourself you won't be able to train the following day. Yet you always do. Rugby is a brutal game but I wouldn't change it for the world. I love it."[142]

Beyond the physical, there's also a mental toughness in Burger. In the modern game, we have seen a growing flexibility in who can be selected for a national team. Burger could have played for South Africa – as, for example, Namibian-born Percy Montgomery did – but this was never going to happen for Burger. He remained committed to his country, though they haven't beaten a Tier One nation since 1991, and – despite his best efforts – was regularly on the wrong end of some very heavy defeats. Nonetheless, he kept coming back and on retirement, left Namibian rugby in a better place than when he began. And such is his love of the sport, it is not hard to envisage him with a future role to play in the development of the game in the country at some point.

There's not always a lot of sense on Twitter, and as noted earlier in this chapter, it can land plenty in trouble. But in Burger's Twitter biography, his few words sum him up perfectly. He says he's a proud Namibian, a retired pro rugby player and farmer, and states perhaps a personal creed that we saw every time he stepped on to the pitch: "The brave may not live forever, but the cautious never live."

ARMAND VAQUERIN

"He was a free man, he didn't like constraints."

VISITORS TO BÉZIERS in the south of France are able to stroll down the Avenue Armand Vaquerin. Should boules be their thing, then they could compete in the Armand Vaquerin annual cup. Or if visiting in the summer months and they prefer rugby, then they could watch teams from all over the world compete in Challenge Armand Vaquerin, now in its 29th year. Or perhaps if they visit the Stade Raoul-Barrière, the home of AS Béziers, they could pose by the statue of Armand Vaquerin that stands outside – a large stone monument, depicting the man himself, muscles bulging, bursting forth from a granite block while holding aloft the *Bouclier de Brennus* (Brennus Shield, the trophy awarded to the winners of the French league) with the number 10, the number of times he won the shield, proudly carved upon it.

The rugby pubs in the centre all have his image, balding, bearded or moustachioed depending on the year, looking down sternly upon their patrons. If an audio accompaniment is required during the visitor's time in the town, then an acclaimed 2018 eight-part podcast series, *Le Canon sur la Tempe*, on his life and times could be the perfect soundtrack.

A full 27 years after his death, Armand Vaquerin still looms large over Béziers.

Yes, it's because of how he was as a player – we'll get to that – and yes, it's because of his shocking, untimely death – and we'll get to that too. But perhaps it is also about what the period in which he played meant to the town.

Béziers is a small town of 75,000 inhabitants, built around a rocky crag beside the River Orb, and is famous for two things, wine and bullfighting, with the normally sedate pace of life become more frenetic during the five-day *Féria* in August, when both can be heartily enjoyed. It might be picturesque but it is poor, suffers relatively high unemployment and is often overlooked for many of its flashier, more illustrious neighbours.

But through the period when Vaquerin played for the club, there was nothing sedate about the town's rugby club, nor was anyone overshadowing their achievements. Between 1971 and 1984, AS Béziers won the French Championship ten times. Before this remarkable purple patch, they had only won it once, in 1961, and they have not triumphed again since then.

Vaquerin was the toughest player in the team, but the players he lined up with might well deserve the title of hardest club team of all time, with him being joined by Alain Estève (aka the 'Beast of Béziers', the tormentor of Bobby Windsor, who could easily have had his own chapter in this book); Michel Palmié, whose career ended with a lifetime ban after punching an opponent and leaving him partially blinded in one eye – an infraction that didn't, however, stop him later taking up a position as an official with the French Rugby Federation;

and other assorted hard nuts including Alain Paco, Jean-Louis Martin, Georges Senal and Olivier Saïsset.

Overseeing this brawn was the brain of Raoul Barrière, a former prop who coached Béziers to six titles between 1971 and 1978. A PE teacher by trade, he adopted coaching and fitness practices more akin to the modern professional era, rather than amateur years of the 1970s. Years ahead of their rivals, the Béziers players trained most days, were weighed each week, had regular blood samples taken and were offered advice on dietary best practice. Barrière, after experiencing the sharp end of South African rugby on a tour there with the French national team, saw the template for success as a ferocious Springbok pack, but with added local *je ne sais quoi*.

The rest of French rugby never stood a chance.

And the cornerstone of this success was Armand Vaquerin, born in 1951 to parents who had fled over the Pyrenees from Franco's Spain, in Sévérac-le-Château, Languedoc, around 90 minutes north of Béziers. He grew up helping in Le Mondial, the bar they owned. He didn't play the game as a child, only picking it up as a teenager – but once he did, he didn't look back. Aged 19, he made his debut for Béziers and the 6', 16-stone loose-head prop quickly established himself in the first XV, making his International debut the following year, aged just 20 years and 10 months. Playing in a position that values canniness and wiles as much as physical strength and playing ability, to be capped so quickly for such a strong team shows just what a good player Vaquerin was.

The same year he first played for his country, he won the first of his French Championships with AS Béziers. The fact that he ended up lifting the famous trophy ten times in total makes him the most successful club player ever to have played in France. It seems unlikely anyone will ever take this remarkable record.

The most successful and perhaps the most feared, for the kindly face belied a player with a brutal ferocity on the pitch.

Fellow hard man of this era – and this book – Bobby Windsor, who found the French of this vintage were the only team to regularly get the better of the Welsh, described Vaquerin as both a "tough guy" and a "headcase".[143]

The Irish too would remember with a shudder their experiences against Vaquerin and his AS Béziers teammates, who filled out most of the French pack in this era. Flanker Stewart McKinney was brought in for his Ireland debut to sort out their scrum and was no angel himself. He freely admits, "Rucking and mauling was my game. I did a lot of stuff on the ground, probably illegally."

But this French team would prove a very different proposition for McKinney and his teammates. "There was aggro in the first couple of scrums. Alain Estève, their second row, was kicking people and it got dirty. When I got the chance later on, I shoed him. I shoed him to hurt him. He was on the ground and he just winked at me. He should have been dead. Estève was one of the toughest bastards around... he was one of five Béziers guys in their pack that day. They were French champions at the time. Fucking mental. Armand Vaquerin was one of them. A loose-head prop. And a total looper..."[144]

The Scots as well were terrorised by Vaquerin and the gang. Sandy Carmichael, even decades after facing him, remembers him as a "mental case".[145]

When not intimidating his opponents, Vaquerin was a mobile prop, especially for this era, with an ability to punch holes in the opposition defence (as well as the occasional opposition face) and a knack for scoring tries. Completely fearless, he took the fight to any opponent, however illustrious or wherever they were, and particularly relished away fixtures and overseas tours.

But off the field, he was different, enjoying drinking with opposition players he'd been smashing into the ground just hours before. "Many of Armand's former adversaries have said a lot of good things about him. All the problems were solved when leaving the field," said Alain Castéran, author of a 2013 biography on Vaquerin.[146]

Vaquerin collected 26 caps for France before a knee injury curtailed his International career in 1980, although he would continue to feature for his beloved AS Béziers until 1986. His illustrious and fulfilling playing career would, however, lead into a troubled and ultimately tragic retirement.

On hanging up his boots, Armand and his wife moved to Mexico, where they worked in tourism near Acapulco for a few years. After returning via Spain to Béziers, he opened a bar, Le Cardiff, a tribute to his battles (and post-match drinks) with the Welsh. The bar proved popular and Vaquerin was a genial host – but this all came to a sudden, shuddering end one night in 1993.

The exact details of what happened have never been proved, but what we do know is that on 10 July 1993 Vaquerin left a party at his own bar, organised in tribute to the 20th anniversary of his first cap for France, after just one drink and headed to a seedier establishment, Le Bar des Amis, on the other side of town. Whilst there, he got into an altercation with another drinker. Apparently, he challenged him to a fight, the man declined, and Vaquerin then pulled out a Smith & Wesson revolver and asked him to play Russian roulette with him. The man promptly exited the bar, leaving Vaquerin still keen to play but not finding any takers. He reportedly shouted, "If you bastards won't play with me, I'll play by myself."

He put a bullet in one of the six chambers, spun the barrel, placed the gun to his temple and pulled the trigger. He shot himself dead.

Armand Vaquerin was 42 years old.

27 years on from his death, the exact events of that night, and the man himself, remain an enigma. The official version, widely reported, is death by Russian roulette, but Alain Castéran paints a picture of a man who didn't have suicidal tendencies: "Armand loved life, was in good shape, he had plans..."[147]

The podcast *Le Canon sur la Tempe* (translated as 'the gun to your head', compelling you to do something) disputes the official version and looks instead at cocaine and organised crime in the region as playing a role in this violent event.

Whatever the details of Vaquerin's premature demise, his legend lives on both in Béziers, where he is still revered, and in the memories of those who had the misfortune to face him.

A talented man, a troubled man, but a true hard man.

As a final postscript to this story, since the days of Vaquerin and company, AS Béziers have struggled. They've not come closing to winning another Championship and have been out of the top flight for over a decade, enduring ongoing financial woes. There was feverish talk of a takeover from an Emirati consortium, with Christophe Dominici acting as a go-between and some of the biggest names in world rugby heading to the town. It has since come to nothing, and the future of the club is looking bleak.

To add to the general bizarreness of the situation, shortly after the deal fell through, Dominici was involved in an incident at a milliner's in Sanary-sur-Mer on the French Riviera, where after requesting a "the most expensive" hat in the shop, he found a Panama to his liking. He wanted to take the hat and pay later, and when his offer was declined by the shopkeeper, a shirtless Dominici became agitated, a melee ensued and the police were called. At the time of writing, an investigation was still underway.

Like some national teams and other famous old clubs around the world – Pontypool in Wales springs to mind, as well as some grand old clubs along the Scottish borders – AS Béziers have found the world of professional rugby a bigger challenge than anything they ever faced on the pitch.

Here's hoping they find some answers soon, and ensure the legacy of the man Armand Vaquerin is backed by the continuation of the club to which he gave everything for so many years.

MARTIN JOHNSON

"He's a genuinely hard man, as mentally strong as he is physically. He doesn't have bad games – it can be somewhat demoralising when you come up against him."

FACTFILE

Full name: Martin Osborne Johnson CBE
Born: 9 March 1970, Solihull, England
Position: Lock
Representative teams: New Zealand U21, England U21, Barbarians, England, British & Irish Lions
Clubs: King Country, Leicester
Nickname: Johnno

THE CROWDS, THE media and the money are just three of the many things that have changed about the Rugby World Cup since it was established in 1987. But one thing that has remained constant is how the Webb Ellis Cup itself has been raised aloft by the skipper of the victorious team. The captain, with one hand on each of the handles, delivers a straight lift and a big smile, as the blazers behind clap/fireworks explode – delete as applicable for whichever era you are watching the final in.

But not in 2003 – when Martin Johnson, the triumphant England captain, took a different approach when handed the trophy by a morose-looking Australian Prime Minister, John Howard. Johnson's huge hands enveloped the trophy, avoiding the handles and treating it almost like a ball, with one clasping its side and the other placed upon its lid. At the special moment, he then lifted it up with a roar, treating the world to a rare view of the base of the trophy, as his teammates behind raised their hands and cheered. With a bloody cut across his nose amplifying his already rugged appearance, it took some time after lifting the trophy for a smile to appear on Johnson's face, and watching the video again, I think it is possible to see the precise moment when the impact of what he and his team had done that day hit home, and the pressure seemed to drift off his shoulders.

Lifting the World Cup in an unpolished, defiant, almost bearlike way might seem an inconsequential thing to some, but for me it neatly sums up the approach to rugby of the man who was England's dominant figure from the end of the amateur era to that glorious night in Sydney. Hugely successful as a player, whether for Leicester, England or the Lions, Johnson's abrasive style of play and no-nonsense approach to opponents, teammates and sometimes even protocol and diplomatic niceties made him unpopular in some quarters. Springbok skipper Corné Krige was firmly in that camp, describing his England counterpart in 2003 as "one of the dirtiest captains in world rugby".

Johnson himself, however, disagrees with the perception that some have of him, stating in his autobiography that "few players have attracted more censure than me. Somehow, unfairly I believe, I have developed a reputation for illegal physical violence on the field of play. I am sure part of it is my size and general appearance; it doesn't help being 6' 7" tall and 19 stone, with one big black eyebrow stuck on the top of a pretty bashed-up face."[148]

Nothing divides opinion likes success, and with few players achieving as much as Johnson did, it is no surprise that he drew criticism. As we'll see, some of it was unfair, but some was justified. What can't be disputed, though, is the enormous impact he had on whatever team was fortunate enough to have him as their leader.

Born in England's Midlands in 1970, he was not immediately marked for greatness. In his late teens, he was on the fringes of the Leicester set-up but it was not until, as noted in the Colin Meads chapter, an opportunity appeared to head to New Zealand and play for King Country in the National Provincial Championship (NPC) that he kick-started his career. The sink-or-swim environment found in the rural heartlands of the Kiwi game improved both his play and his confidence; so much so that he appeared three times for the New Zealand U21 team. Having met a local girl who he would later marry, a different path might have made Johnson a full All Black. But at the end of his two years down under, he returned to Leicester, quickly broke into their first team and would never look back.

Leicester would be his only club in England and between his first appearance in 1989 and his last in 2005, he played in 362 games for them. He was club captain from 1997 to his retirement and led the team to a Pilkington Cup final victory in 1997, four successive Premiership titles from 1999–2002 and back-to-back Heineken Cup wins in 2001 and 2002. The heart of this dynasty was a relentless pack of forwards, with Johnson the ace, but also joined by other talented and tough teammates: Neil Back, Richard Cockerill, Lewis Moody and Darren Garforth, to name but a few.

A fixture between this Leicester team and Armand Vaquerin's 1970s Béziers outfit would have been something to behold – if a referee brave enough to take charge could have been found!

Johnson made his International debut in 1993 and would go on to make 84 appearances for England, 39 of them as captain. In his time wearing the red rose, he won five Five/Six Nations Championships before leading the team to their greatest ever moment – winning the 2003 Rugby World Cup in Australia. No other northern hemisphere team has won a World Cup, either before or since.

Johnson played on the edge and never swerved from a challenge, however intimidating, as the South Africans found to their cost during the 1997 Lions tour. He'd toured in 1993 (as we've noted, as a replacement for Wade Dooley, profiled earlier in the book) having only played for England once, but by 1997 he was an established figure as a player – though significantly less so as a captain. Despite some strong contenders in the shape of Ieuan Evans, Keith Wood and Rob Wainwright, he was named the skipper for the first Lions tour of the professional era and was the first since World War II to be appointed without first leading his country.

The manager for that tour, Ian McGeechan, debated Johnson's relative lack of experience as a captain with the other coaches, but saw in him several other key attributes. "Johnson, I always believed, was something else. I was coaching at Northampton at the time, and Leicester were our big rivals. Games between the two were always massive. So I saw first-hand the impact Johnson had on his own team and the impact he had on the opposition."

He continued, "After Martin was chosen, he even went off to do some public relations and media training, although the essential gift he brought on the pitch and into the team environment was to be the man himself. It was also the first time I really became set on having a physically imposing figure leading the Lions. I felt that psychologically it would unnerve the opposition to arrive for the toss under the stands before the game, and to see a giant of a man waiting for him, beetle-browed and scowling, rather than some weedy back!"[149]

McGeechan would later report that he heard "on good authority" that when Johnson and Gary Teichmann, the South African captain, met before the first Test for the coin toss, the Springbok skipper wasn't able to look his opposite number in the eye.

This is Gary Teichmann, one of the most successful Springbok captains ever, who himself was 6' 5" and 15st 7lbs.

Johnson, as tour captain, was no fan of theatrics, needless speeches or grandstanding. He let other senior players talk, but when he did make comment, the team listened. One of his strengths was making the right call on the pitch, even when under extreme pressure, and he was happy to put his confidence in his teammates. In the first Test he barely called any line-outs for himself; his partner at lock, Irishman Jeremy Davidson, had the beating of the Springbok jumpers in the middle, so he let him lead at the set piece.

With his leadership, physicality and ability to deliver excellence at the set piece, rucks and mauls, the Lions never took a step back and notched up a historic 2-1 series victory.

Four years later, he would again be selected to captain the Lions, this time in Australia – the first ever player selected to lead two separate tours. This time, however, there would be no series victory, with it going down to the final frantic minutes of the third Test and the Australians just holding out to take the game 29-23 and the series 2-1.

The veneer of the hard man was peeled away by this bitter defeat, and several years later Johnson wrote, "The deflation was sudden and horrible. All that we had worked for, all our dreams, all gone in a matter of seconds. I was close to tears – for the guys that had worked so hard, for the supporters who had spent so much time and money following us and who, to an extent, we had let down. It was my last time in a Lions shirt, a dreadful memory that will live with me forever."[150]

Johnson would have a few other disappointments in his glittering playing career, but nothing as agonising as this Lions series defeat.

Putting aside his immense ability as a player and a leader, there were moments where his ultra-physical approach to the game would land him in hot water and, despite his protestations that his rugged appearance marked him unfairly in the eyes of referees, disciplinary issues ran like a thread all through his career.

All Black scrum half Justin Marshall received a punch from behind in a 1997 Test match that affected his hearing, with Johnson receiving a one-game ban and the act being labelled by Kiwi coach John Hart as "outright thuggery from someone who should know better".[151]

In 1999, John Leslie of Scotland had Johnson's studs on his neck at a ruck in a Calcutta Cup match, which Scottish Sports Minister Sam Galbraith would describe as an "absolutely appalling act" and for which the England man received a yellow card. The same year, he landed a punch on another Scot, his Lions teammate Doddie Weir, during a Barbarians v. Leicester game at Twickenham.

Then there was the cup game against Saracens in 2000 when he both punched England colleague Julian White and put a knee into Australian stand-off Duncan McRae, damaging his ribs. He received a 35-day ban from the RFU, though luckily for Johnson it just happened to end the day before England's Six Nations Championship opener against Wales in Cardiff.

In the 2001 Heineken Cup Final, Johnson was sin-binned after punching Stade Français No. 8 Christophe Juillet in the face after the Frenchman held on to his shirt.

The following year he got a three-week ban for smacking Saracens and Scotland hooker Robbie Russell in an off-the-ball incident.

And so on, and so forth.

In his autobiography, Johnson devotes a chapter to his reputation – entitled 'Terminator in Shorts', apparently what his wife calls him – and analyses all these incidents. He admits he is "no angel" but finds reason or at least mitigation for this rap sheet. For the punch on Marshall, for example, he says the scrum half had "come offside to compete for the ball a couple of times" and his connection with him was "a stiff arm – not even a proper punch."[152]

When it came to Robbie Russell, he "was right in my face, all aggression and grappling arms" and "it was not intended as much of a punch – it was more of a slap."[153]

McRae's ribs were broken because "I charged into the ruck, and my knee caught his body hard. At that pace, and with so many bodies around, you can't control which part of your body comes into contact with which part of your opponent's."[154]

And so on, and so forth.

It wasn't only opponents that he clashed with. He also created a minor international incident in Dublin in 2003, at the Grand Slam decider between Ireland and England. Emerging first from the changing rooms, Johnson led the team out and lined them up on the side that was reserved for the home team. When this was pointed out to Johnson, he refused to move and the crowd began to go wild as the officials' gesticulations became increasingly desperate. Arriving on the pitch, the Irish team refused to stand where the away team should have gone, so moved to the right of the visitors, leaving one half of the red carpet unoccupied and forcing the Irish President Mary McAleese to dirty her shoes by trudging along the muddy turf to shake hands with the Ireland players.

To add salt to the wound, England won the game 42-6, and Johnson's reputation as something of a pantomime villain in parts of the rugby world grew further. Despite what some might have thought – and there was a media storm about the incident – it was more a faux pas from Johnson than a planned act of provocation, although the RFU did issue a "full and unreserved apology" to President McAleese post-match.

It's hard for any real rugby fan to disagree that Johnson was a fantastic player, although your view of his career as a whole, discipline and all, is likely to depend on where your team allegiances lie. But for those who have played either with or against him, the respect is undimmed.

Chris Wyatt, the Llanelli and Wales lock, admits that Johnson would "not be my favourite person" but agrees that "as captain and a second row, you have to pay him the utmost respect. He has not survived at the top for 10 years for nothing. As a leader, there is no one to compare with him. He would not ask his players to do anything he was not prepared to take on himself – he leads by example and he is someone others are ready to follow."[155]

Doddie Weir, both a teammate for the Lions and an opponent when in Scottish colours, has a dual perspective on him. "We roomed together with the Lions and he was forceful as a captain both on and off the field, but he could be a quiet bloke as well and he thinks about the game a lot. But he will stand up and be counted and there is nothing a player likes more than to follow a captain who leads from the front. He has utter respect. He is dedicated to the game and his record speaks for itself."[156]

Weir continues, "Mind you, I have been on the other side, playing for Scotland, and he is a large handful to play against, but dirty doesn't come into it. He's always such an utter joy to play against – if you like the physical stuff."

Danny Grewcock, the Bath and England lock, is full of admiration. "He's just unrelenting. No matter what you throw at him, he's always there, he's always strong and he just keeps on going. He's one of those players who, as long as he's on the pitch, you never feel you can beat. It's not like, 'Look, his confidence has gone, he's shot now, he'll go quiet.' He just gets louder and bigger than ever. If you're up against him, you know you've got to play your best just to compete.

"He's a genuinely hard man, as mentally strong as he is physically. He doesn't have bad games – it can be somewhat demoralising when you come up against him at club level. I can't think of anyone in English sport, bar maybe Steve Redgrave, who can match what he's achieved over such a long period of time."[157]

After his retirement in 2005, the post-playing career of Johnson contained a major surprise. He took over as England manager in 2008, and although his team won the Six Nations in 2011, he resigned after a disappointing and, at times, chaotic World Cup later that year. I say it was a surprise not because his tenure in charge didn't work out – great players don't always make great coaches and he came into the top job in English rugby without any managerial experience – but because, if anything, this hardest of hard men as a player was too soft on his players as a coach.

He gave his players a lot of leeway in terms of behaviour, and was repaid with a stream of distracting incidents at the World Cup in New Zealand. This included members of the team attending an event call the 'Mad Midget Weekender', where dwarf wrestling was taking place; a police caution for Manu Tuilagi after he jumped off a ferry about to berth at the Auckland Ferry Terminal and swam to a nearby pier; and the ejection of centre Mike Tindall from England's elite player squad after the tournament following allegations of inappropriate behaviour in New Zealand.

Johnson also committed too long to coaches and players, several of whom were his former colleagues, who could no longer deliver, and his conservative approach ultimately saw England exit to France in the quarter-finals.

Having emerged from the amateur era, when there was no social media, no camera phones and a greater acceptance of high jinks and big nights out, Johnson never instilled the hard-nosed attitude he had as a player into the team that he coached. On being quizzed on the furore around Mike Tindall, he dismissed the story as "rugby player drinks beer shocker" – he was probably right, but that's not the way the media world works now.

Ultimately, with his trusting, laid-back approach, he allowed the players plenty of rope and eventually it was Johnson that was hanged, as he resigned in November 2011.

Since departing from the top job at Twickenham, he has not worked again in rugby coaching, instead keeping busy with some punditry, after-dinner speaking, business motivation and a growing interest in cycling. For a man that proved such a leader, it seems a low-key way of marking time, but perhaps he's won all the battles he needs to fight. English rugby has never known a figure like him, and perhaps never will again.

Perhaps we should give the last word to Lions legend Ian McGeechan, twice a playing tourist and four times a coach. Throughout his writings, he repeatedly returns to the concept of the 'Test-match animal' as being what makes a good player a great one.

His definition of this term is a player that is "never prepared to be second. He knows what is required and he does it again, again, again, and he does it in such a physical, determined and focused way, he is never going to be beaten. His instinct is just a little bit more ruthless than the others... It is about animal instinct. He is there not just for survival, but for control."[158]

McGeechan lists those who have had this 'Test-match animal' status: J P R Williams, Gareth Edwards, Gavin Hastings, Jonny Wilkinson and Ieuan Evans are there, as is hard man Scott Gibbs and several others McGeechan played with and coached between 1974 and 2009, but for him the "greatest example of a Test-match animal" was Martin Johnson, and I doubt a higher compliment could possibly be paid in modern rugby.

BRIAN THOMAS

"He came over to toss the coin before kick-off and stood there almost blocking out the light, with a huge black eye – somehow sustained in his own dressing room."

FACTFILE

Full name: Brian Thomas
Born: 18 May 1940, Neath, Wales
Died: 9 July 2012, Neath, Wales
Position: Lock
Representative team: Wales
Clubs: Cambridge University RFC, Neath
Nickname: the Ayatollah

THERE WAS AN unusual illness that would affect a small portion of the south Wales populace through the 1970s and 1980s. It would flare up on Friday evenings, get consistently worse until 2.30 on Saturday afternoon, then magically clear up. It would centre on those who were required to travel up the M4 and had some very high-profile International rugby players as its victims. Doctors and physios were perplexed but fans recognised its impact as soon as the depleted visiting teams were announced over the tannoy at the Gnoll. This curious outbreak was known as Neath Flu, its results were often brutal defeats and one of its root causes both as a player and a manager was Brian Thomas, one of the fiercest players ever to step onto a pitch in Wales, and one who lost little of his fire when he swapped his boots for a blazer and tie.

His legacy still looms large over rugby in the south Wales town, another that has struggled in recent years to navigate the world of professionalism and the regional game, but what Thomas achieved, and how he put the name Neath on the map for world rugby, continues to resonate for many rugby fans around the world.

For a young Gareth Llewellyn, just breaking into the Neath team and still to win the first of 92 caps for Wales, Thomas the coach gave him one of the sharpest memories of his fledgling career. Aged just 19, in the summer of 1988 he was with Neath on a preseason tour of the south of France.

"Let's just say the trip was of its time," said Llewellyn, recalling it 32 years later to a Wales Online reporter. "I was only a kid, so it was an eye-opener in every respect. Brian Thomas, who was running the rugby side of things at Neath at the time, had told us beforehand the tour would be character-building, and so it proved."[159]

The day after a match, they visited a farm. Many of the team were farmers themselves, so they enjoyed the tour and then a nice outdoor lunch with several bottles of pastis to loosen everyone up. Once everyone was suitably refreshed, the visit had a change of pace – they were led to a bullring and told they could go in and have a go. Six were brave enough, thinking they would only encounter calves, but quickly regretted the decision when a large adult bull was let in, with steel balls on the end of its huge horns to offer at least some protection if you were caught.

Llewellyn continued the story: "The boys were creeping out from behind the safety barriers until Andrew Kembery decided to edge a bit further. The bull, in the meantime, was doing everything you'd seen in cartoons – scraping the dust back with his hooves, bowing his head and snorting.

"I thought to myself, 'If that bull runs, Kembers is not going to make it back to safety.' With that, the bull took off.

"Instead of trying to reach safety, Kembery panicked and pulled up the cloak in front of him and got absolutely flattened. He was knocked off his feet and had a huge gouge down his chest where a steel ball had hit him, which meant he couldn't take part in the game at the weekend.

"The French guys who were watching were just laughing at it all."

By this time, even Thomas was getting concerned that his afternoon of team bonding was getting seriously out of hand, and ordered his players out of the ring. But the story didn't quite end there. Prop Brian Williams, before he could exit, was next to be lined up by the bull. Now, in targeting Williams, a superbly physical and tough player, unlucky to win just five caps for his country and someone who could perhaps have had his own chapter in this book, the bull had made a bad choice of opponent.

The Pembrokeshire farmer, rather than running away, tackled the bull around the neck, and it began charging around the ring with the prop holding on tight. He eventually fell off but then got back up, and used all his skills of animal husbandry to calm the bull. The French were astonished at what they saw.

Those who knew this Neath team, or the iron will Thomas instilled into them, would not have been so surprised.

Born at the top of the Neath Valley and having attended the town's grammar school, Thomas headed to Cambridge University to study metallurgy and win three Blues. Alongside his academic endeavours and varsity rugby, he was playing for his home town club. He would win his first of 21 Wales caps against England in 1963 and was part of the successful Wales side that won the Five Nations in 1964, 1965 and 1966.

Coming in at 6' 4" and 17st, Thomas was a good line-out jumper and an expert in spoiling opposition possession, but it was in the maul that he excelled. The pack leader for both

Wales and Neath, he was able to add his immense physical strength and his canny rugby brain to give his teams a huge advantage up front.

His jumping ability was tested to the extreme in his second game for Wales, a 6-0 win over Scotland, which featured 111 line-outs, neatly divided between 55 in the first half and 56 in the second. It was estimated that 38 of the 80 minutes were spent preparing for or taking line-outs. And there was no lifting in the line-out in those days.

As Wales celebrated a valuable away Five Nations win, many who saw the match were left unimpressed. In the *Daily Express*, Pat Marshall was particularly forthright. "This was power-rugby, brutally bludgeoned up and down the touchlines by two brutish packs with kicking scrum halves yapping at their heels. It has no part in the pattern of British rugby, where quickness of wit and fleetness of foot still counts for more than brawn supported by an educated boot. Rowlands won a tactical victory, but it was no victory for rugby."

Clive Rowlands, the Wales skipper, was cheerfully unrepentant, for his game plan had worked. "No, I was never at any time tempted to open the game up and let my backs make the running. That's what Scotland were praying we'd do."[160]

Whilst picking up the winning habit for his country, Thomas was developing a hard-man reputation for his club, where he would soon become captain. His Neath team were as intimidating as they were successful, winning the 1966/67 Welsh Championship, and he was at the heart of some ferocious performances.

There's a tale, told in the excellent *Hard Men of Welsh Rugby*, that during a local derby against Aberavon at the Gnoll, he emerged from a ruck with blood streaming out of his mouth. At this point a Neath supporter shouted, "Aberavon! You'd better count your forwards! I think he's eaten one of you!"[161]

Phil Bennett recalls the effect that Thomas had on him, coming to play Neath at the Gnoll as the 19-year-old captain of Llanelli. "Brian Thomas was an enormous man who knew the effect his presence had on young 11-stone flyweights like myself. He came over to toss the coin before kick-off and stood there almost blocking out the light, with a huge black eye, somehow sustained in his own dressing room.

"He laughed in my face. 'You! What's wrong? Have Llanelli run out of grown men to captain their team these days?' I felt intimidated and not surprisingly we lost the match."[162]

Bennett's experience wouldn't have been unusual, and Thomas' reputation with the press and officials might have caught up with him in 1965 in a bizarre incident following a win over England. With Richard Burton and Elizabeth Taylor in the crowd, Wales won 14-3 but afterwards English forward Geoff Frankcom claimed he had been bitten on the cheek by a Welsh forward. Initially Frankcom was hazy as to who his assailant had been but at the post-match dinner, he reportedly leapt up, pointing at Brian Thomas and shouting, "It's him, it's him! He just refused a third helping of beef because of what he ate this afternoon!"

There was no proof that Thomas was the culprit, nor was he cited, but he was the only player from the victorious team to be dropped for the next game, and he didn't play any of the remaining Wales fixtures that season.

I guess we will never know, but it is said that his pre-match meal was a pound of grapes, so perhaps feeling a little peckish mid-match wouldn't be that surprising.

He made his final appearance for Wales in 1969, just as the likes of Barry John and Gareth Edwards were emerging, and retired from playing for Neath after leading them to win the inaugural Welsh Cup in 1972. Thomas took a decade out of the game and, as a trained metallurgist, worked for British Steel in senior-management roles across south Wales, including at the plants at Trostre and Velindre, where numerous Welsh Internationals also worked. He was always very supportive in granting precious time off for training and matches.

But the siren call of Neath couldn't be resisted for too long, and in 1982 he returned to the Gnoll as the first ever team manager appointed by a Welsh club.

What Thomas, his fellow coaches and players at Neath achieved was nothing short of a revolution. He managed to turn the 'Welsh All Blacks' into a unit as effective and feared as their New Zealand namesakes. They progressed each year before really hitting their stride in 1986/87, when they would win the first of four consecutive Welsh Championships. The 1988/89 season was particularly remarkable, with the club setting two new world records for a club side – 1,917 points and 345 tries.

Lyn Jones, later a coach with Neath, the Ospreys and now the Russian national side, was a flanker at the club during this period and recalls the importance of the manager. "During that great spell in the 80s, Brian Thomas was all about recruiting people with the right character. If they didn't have the right values that aligned with how he saw the club being – ferociously hard-working and determined – then he wouldn't sign them, even if they were good enough to play for Wales."[163]

His management of Neath coincided with the last notable club v. country games and the Gnoll would always be a cauldron for visiting nations, most notably in 1994 when the Springboks came to town. The tourists, with a team including the likes of Kobus Wiese, Joel Stransky, James Dalton, Tiaan Strauss and Mark Andrews, came away with a 16-13 win, but even for these tough characters, that November night in south Wales must have come as a shock.

For the full 80 minutes the teams shoved, kicked and punched each other, the team doctors working overtime as players came on and off the pitch with all sorts of bandages and stitches holding them together and one fight rolled from one 22 to the other 22.

To say the referee lost control would be inaccurate – he never had it to begin with.

Post-match, South Africa called for Neath to be banned from hosting tour matches, with Tiaan Strauss, who had had his nose broken after a foolish attempt to poleaxe the bull-taming Brian Williams, saying, "I think they went on the field to fight us."

Brian Thomas responded bluntly, "I don't worry about punching and kicking. That's all part of the game."[164]

This 'Battle of the Gnoll' came two years after the manager of a visiting Australia team, Bob Dwyer – whose team had come away with their own narrow victory – accused the home side of engaging in some underhand testicle-grabbing antics. So much so that he labelled Neath the 'bag-snatching capital of the universe', that being the Australian slang term for that particular 'manoeuvre'.

Midweek games between major nations and club sides really are a thing of the past, and looking back on these fixtures, it's hard not to feel a little pang for what the game has lost. Packed grounds in provincial towns giving local boys the chance to stick it to some global superstars. Sure, most of the time the visitors came away triumphant, often handsomely so; but sometimes, just sometimes, it went the other way. When it did, the men that had made it happen were legends for life.

Few people in any sport could be said to have had as big an influence on their town as Brian Thomas did on Neath. Even today, with the first-class club merged with bitter rivals to form the Ospreys in 2003 and the semi-professional outfit struggling financially in the second tier of Welsh rugby, if you say "Neath" to most rugby people, they will instantly see a black jersey, a Maltese cross and perhaps a grizzled face to wear it.

Brian Thomas was an intimidating enforcer of a forward and brought this quality, allied with fast and skilful backs, to create a legendary Neath club team – the likes of which may never be seen again.

SÉBASTIEN CHABAL

"They told us to act like it was a war, to show them that we were ready for a good fight."

FACTFILE

Full name: Sébastien Chabal
Born: 8 December 1977, Valence, Drôme, France
Positions: No. 8, Lock, Flanker
Representative team: France
Clubs: Valence Sportif, Club Sportif Bourgoin-Jallieu, Sale Sharks, Racing Métro, Lyon
Nicknames: the Caveman, Attila, Rasputin, Seabass, the Anaesthetist

THERE'S ALWAYS A buzz around the Hong Kong Sevens, the world's premier tournament for the short version of the game. The stands are packed with boisterous fans, often in fancy dress, and the beer flows as easily as the tries. It's not quite anything goes, but certainly there are few sights across the three days of action that would raise too many eyebrows.

That was, perhaps, until the 2019 edition, when to the delight and slight puzzlement of the raucous South Stand at the Hong Kong Stadium, the subject of this chapter – dressed as a caveman, complete with animal pelts across his chest – belted out a version of 'I'm Gonna Be (500 Miles)' by The Proclaimers. Flanked by three men wearing leopard skins, fake moustaches and pretending to play musical instruments, the performance wouldn't get too many marks for his singing, but would receive extra credit for his enthusiasm.

The commentators, before dissolving into fits of laughter, expressed their delight: "Things I never thought I'd see on a Friday afternoon in Hong Kong... Sébastien Chabal singing [laughter]. I think I'm done. I'm dead. French hard man! [more laughter] He's still a hard man, the former French star, but when the men in the leopard-print jumpsuits aren't the story. Only in Hong Kong! Crank it up. That's just the best... [dissolves into laughter]."[165]

This performance was part of his work for Marriott Hotels, promoting their new loyalty points scheme. Other videos in this partnership see the 6' 3", 18-stone Frenchman dressed as a maid, a chef and in full drag, complete with wig and heels.

The chief creative officers of Ogilvy, the advertising agency that created the campaign, said: "We chose Sébastien because of his continued passion for the game of rugby, even after his retirement. During his playing years, his ability to manoeuvre creatively around the pitch and inspire fans is perfectly aligned with the Marriott Hotels ethos of innovation, creativity, dynamism, and inventiveness."[166]

Of course it is.

Helping sell hotel stays to business travellers is a long way from the 2007 World Cup, when Chabal glared and snarled his way through a rare challenge to the haka that preceded a famous French victory over the All Blacks. But then the Chabal story has always been a complex one.

Born in Valence, south-east France, to a working-class family with no interest in rugby, he didn't play the game until he was 16 so there was no fast-track through an academy or age-grade representative games for him, unlike most who reach the top level of the sport. After leaving school he played rugby only at weekends, spending his week as a milling machine operator for an engineering firm. It was only in 1998, aged 21, that he joined Valence Sportif in the lower reaches of the French rugby pyramid and not till two years later, when he joined Bourgoin in the top flight, that he became a fully-fledged professional. His uncompromising tackling quickly helped mark him out as a ferocious player, and he picked up the nickname 'the Anaesthetist' on account of its effects on opponents.

Chabal's International debut was aged 23 in France's 2000 Six Nations win over Scotland, and he established himself in that tournament as a solid, though not spectacular, cog across the back five of the pack in an inconsistent French team. He went to the 2003 World Cup, where *Les Bleus* came fourth, but was not a regular starter in the big games, being relied upon more as an impact player off the bench.

In 2004, he moved across the Channel and joined Sale Sharks. He proved popular at the Manchester outfit and spent five seasons in England, winning the Premiership in 2006 and enjoying some memorable performances in European competition, including a Challenge Cup triumph in 2005. Coached by fellow Frenchman Philippe Saint-André, who he had worked with at Bourgoin, he played the best rugby of his career in England. Lining up alongside the likes of razor-sharp backs Jason Robinson, Charlie Hodgson, Mark Cueto and Mark Taylor, he was the lynchpin of the forward pack. Fans loved his strong running and fearsome tackling and were known to wear T-shirts showing Chabal's face over a skull and crossbones, with the slogan 'Cha-bad to the bone' written underneath.

Whilst in England, he was only shown a modest three yellow cards, although in 2006 he received a red card and a five-week ban for stamping on Lawrence Dallaglio whilst playing for Sale versus Wasps.

But whilst settled and happy in England, there were aspects of the local culture he was less keen on. Predictably, as a proud Frenchman, this centred on the food. "It's a very different way of life. There's no getting away from that. The weather's bad. It rains a lot. Above all, I find the food bizarre. I hardly ever eat English food. My wife and I share the cooking at home. I cook lasagne, boeuf bourguignon, anything really. And when we go out, we look for French restaurants. I don't think much of the English food I have tried. I certainly don't like fish and chips! It's all a question of taste, I suppose. I know the English think it's bizarre we eat snails and frogs' legs and steak tartare."[167]

The big change in his life came in 2005 with the birth of his daughter. It's not unusual for someone to gain a different perspective on life when they become a parent. And yes, I have no doubt that welcoming little Lily Rose into the family made a huge impact on Chabal. But it wasn't the baby that altered the course of his career.

It was the growth of his hair and beard.

A pre-fatherhood Chabal had sported a fairly nondescript short back and sides (Google the photos – you'll barely recognise him!) but when his wife got pregnant, he resolved to let his hair and beard grow until the baby arrived. Once the nappy changes and night feeds were well underway, as his wife liked it, the hirsute look remained. Already an imposing physical specimen, the combination of the flowing black hair, the long beard and the dark piercing eyes made him one of the most instantly recognisable and popular rugby players in the world.

With the image change came the attention – Chabalmania – and with that, the money. By the end of the 2007 World Cup, he was the world's highest-earning rugby player, bringing home more than Dan Carter, Brian O'Driscoll, Jonny Wilkinson or any other player you wish to name from this time.

But before we get into that World Cup and the crazy world that Chabal began to inhabit, let's rewind to the summer before the tournament when, in just a few games, he jumped from someone a series of French coaches had never fully trusted to being a talisman for not just the team, but the whole country.

The marker was put down just 30 seconds into the first of two Tests away in New Zealand, when a high, looping pass came into midfield, giving Chabal the chance to select his target. A split second after All Black flanker Chris Masoe caught the ball, he was smashed into by 'the Caveman' and unceremoniously dumped onto the floor, where he spilled the ball. The Kiwi, himself a tough character, staggered a little when he eventually got to his feet and gave a little rueful smile as his teammates checked on him.

The video of this big hit and Chabal triumphantly flicking back his hair afterwards, looking like the toughest pony you'll ever see, was shown on repeat that week in France and New Zealand, becoming an early YouTube sensation, and to this day it remains a textbook example of how to line up and execute a very hard but legal tackle.

Seven days later in the second Test, ball in hand and short of options on either side of him, Chabal decided to take the direct route through All Black Ali Williams, whose jaw was broken in several places while trying to impede Chabal's progress. A big hit on Williams and another big hit on YouTube.

This further enhanced Chabal's hard-man reputation, but also had a more unexpected impact: it led to Williams publishing a cookbook. The Kiwi flanker had his jaw wired and missed six weeks of action, and he put out a video plea for soup recipes, complete with a special email address: soupforali@allblacks. com. He received over 1,000 and ended up releasing a book with 140 of the best, *Soup for Ali: Recipes that rescued Ali Williams*. Still available in all good New Zealand bookshops, I'm sure. And yes, he did send a signed copy to the man who caused it all.

The final act in Chabal's big summer in 2007 was a superb, decisive try in a win over England at Twickenham. Not long off the bench, and with ten minutes left to go, his pace found him some space in the England half. He brushed off two would-be tacklers before Josh Lewsey tried to stop him near the line, but Lewsey went too high and couldn't stop Chabal crashing over the try line.

This trilogy of performances saw Chabal arrive at the World Cup as a big star. Whilst still operating mainly as a substitute, his face and Neanderthal image was across billboards, adverts, magazine covers and newspaper front pages. A puppet was made of him for France's version of *Spitting Image*, *Les Guignols de l'Info* and he was voted not just the sexiest man at the World Cup but the sexiest man in France. When he appeared on the pitch, French fans shouted, "Mmmm... Chabal!" in reference to an advertisement for '100 per cent French beef', which carries the tag line "Mmmm... Charal!"

A *Times* article breathlessly described what they perceived as his appeal to his countrywomen: "The Frenchwoman – she's sophisticated, she's cultured, she never gets fat. Apparently she also has a thing for old-fashioned caveman appeal, if the recent popularity of Sébastien Chabal is anything to go by... he is credited with bringing thousands of women – *les Chabalistes* – to the game."[168]

Chabal really was the face of the 2007 World Cup, and he added to his reputation with a try from the halfway line against Namibia in a group-stage encounter, where he accelerated between three defenders, then held off two tacklers before scoring in the right corner.

His popularity with his countrymen and women was further enhanced when at a press conference he was asked if he could take a question in English, a language he is fluent in. He replied, in English, "No, we are in France. We speak French," before standing up and walking out, instantly ending the session.

For a long time, France coach Bernard Laporte seemed immune to Chabal's charms, either leaving him on the bench, or using him at flanker rather than his preferred position of No. 8. But in that heady autumn of 2007, he began to see the player differently: "If something is happening around Sébastien, it is because he is performing on the field. He gives confidence to others. We don't take any notice of publicity. We have selected him for his speed and his explosiveness."[169]

And for a few weeks, it did indeed look like something very special was happening for *Les Bleus*. France had a famous victory over New Zealand in a quarter-final in Cardiff, the last game of Jerry Collins' International career. The tone for this triumph was set when, during the haka, the French advanced to within touching distance of the New Zealanders. It was an electric, spontaneous response and not a pre-planned statement, Chabal told *The Sunday Times* ten years later.

"We had not prepared to react to the haka in that way but just before going out on to the pitch they told us to act like it was a war, to show them that we were ready for a good fight," he insisted.[170]

But France's tournament would come to an abrupt halt in the semi-finals, where the hosts lost 14-9 to England. On the final whistle, Chabal slumped to the turf in tears, the photos of which became some of the most famous of the whole tournament. The English papers were unsympathetic – '*Le Miserable*' and 'Not too big to cry' (*Daily Mail*) and 'Chabal, the caveman who cried the tears of a boy...' (*The Daily Telegraph*) were amongst the photo captions.

His World Cup adventure may have been over, but Chabal emerged from the tournament a huge star and had over 20 commercial endorsements, including Currency Fair, Pokerstars, Beats by Dre and SEAT. We don't have enough pages to run through them all, but the one for international currency transfer company Currency Fair was perhaps the most eye-catching as in the adverts he played a fairy, complete with wings and a wand, who bursts into people's houses before they can use an inferior rival.

Yet whilst his profile was sky high and the off-the-pitch earnings were significant, Chabal's playing career was now set into an inexorable decline. After five years in England, he returned to France to join Paris club Racing Métro, signing a three-year contract at a reported €1 million a year. He won a Six Nations Grand Slam in 2010, though had lost his place in the starting line-up so featured again mainly as a substitute, and just a year later an ignominious defeat to Italy at the end of a disappointing tournament would be the last time he pulled on an International jersey.

He flirted seriously with joining a rugby league outfit in Australia but in the end demurred, and in 2012 left Paris to join Lyon in the second tier of French rugby. In his final season before retiring, he ended on a high by helping Lyon get promoted to the top division. He also proved there was a little bit of the old fire in the belly still, by landing a knockout blow on Agen No. 8 Marc Giraud. Now aged 36, Chabal was pulled back from a maul by Giraud, and he turned and stuck one right on the jaw of his opposite number, who collapsed to the floor unconscious. No serious damage was caused, but Chabal received a three-week suspension and the video of the altercation quickly racked up several million views on YouTube.

Chabal played his last game in 2014, and in contrast to the Chabalmania of a few years earlier, the rugby press greeted the news with either a shrug or some vitriol.

French newspaper *Midi Olympique* claimed that Chabal would be remembered for "a look, some nicknames, some adverts and a little bit of rugby."[171] Sarah Mockford of *Rugby World* said in a 2012 article, "Many years from now a rugby historian will chronicle the evolution of the game in the early 21st century and wonder how it was that Chabal fooled so many people for so long."[172] Conor Heneghan of Joe.ie in Ireland had this to say on his career: "He might be one of the most recognisable faces in rugby, but it was often his rugged appearance as opposed to his performances that earned him such fame and notoriety."[173]

So where does that leave Sébastien Chabal? I don't think he was a truly great player and I think if we were to rank the men in this book in order of toughness, he would come somewhere near the bottom – although in the spring of 2020 he did see off a particularly tough opponent, COVID-19, after the virus had laid him out for "a good week or so".

That's not to say he didn't have his moments – just ask Ali Williams. He was decent with the ball in hand, had good pace for a big man and was a superb physical specimen – in addition to the height and weight, he had a remarkably low body-fat ratio of just 7%, the kind of figure usually found in champion cyclists, rather than a player in the engine room of the scrum. And you don't win 62 caps for France just because you have a beard and long hair.

Chabal is a product of the modern game. It's a short-term career and perhaps doing a normal job for a few years early in life taught him the importance of maximising the opportunities that came his way. Who can blame him? Whilst it might be hard to imagine Bobby Windsor dressed as a fairy to advertise moving money around the world, considering the travails he had providing for his family during his career, who is to say he would have said no to such an offer?

And whatever the press and some fans may have thought, Chabal remains an incredibly high-profile figure in the world of rugby. He is a regular on French television, still has a host of endorsements beyond just the Marriott gig that saw him doing karaoke at the Hong Kong Sevens, and runs his own clothing range, Ruckfield ("represents all the codes and values of rugby, be it elegance, toughness, sharing, conviviality") and a winery (naturally), among myriad other projects.

Also, perhaps most intriguingly, he is Christopher *'Highlander'* Lambert's co-star in a crime thriller called *Dirty Cash* – tag line "when you cross the line, there's no limit" – that was in pre-production in the summer of 2020.

So, from machine operating to the silver screen, there could be many more chapters still to come for Sébastien Chabal, a very modern rugby hard man.

WEARY DUNLOP

"A lighthouse of sanity in a universe of madness and suffering."

CAPTAIN NAKAZAWA OF the Imperial Japanese Army had received his orders: the hospital was to be cleared in ten minutes. After a brutal 13-month campaign, the Dutch-British-Australian-American forces had capitulated and he had no desire to spend any longer than necessary on his task. The instruction was simple – everyone out. As the Allied servicemen and women limped, stumbled or were wheeled out of No. 1 Allied General Hospital Bandung in Java (modern day Indonesia) and into captivity under the advancing Japanese, it became clear that this wasn't going to be possible for every patient.

Leading Aircraftman Bill Griffiths of the Royal Air Force had lost his sight and both his hands as well as breaking both of his legs in a bomb blast and was clinging to life on the operating table when Nakazawa entered. A cursory glance at the shattered body of the 18 year old from Blackburn, Lancashire and the Japanese officer nodded to one of his men. Wordlessly he understood what his superior wanted, raised his bayonet and was about to lunge when the Australian commander of the hospital stepped between the blade and young Griffiths.

"If you are going to do that, you must go through me first," he said.[174]

Nakazawa and the army doctor, one Lieutenant-Colonel Dunlop, glared at each other for what must have felt like an age to those in the room. But, despite having the power, it was the Japanese officer who blinked first. He ordered the bayonet be lowered and said the severely wounded would be allowed to leave. The hospital would be cleared, but on Dunlop's and not Nakazawa's terms.

Into Prisoner of War camps would go Dunlop and the 1,300+ patients and staff of the military hospital. This was March 1942, and over three years of cruelty, humiliation, epidemics, forced labour, overcrowding and public executions would await them. But a rare beacon in this misery would be Dunlop, who showed time and time again the bravery he displayed in that operating theatre. By the time the Japanese were defeated, many more servicemen would owe their lives to this remarkable man.

Ten years earlier, his life had been very different.

'Weary' had picked up his nickname as a play on his last name – "tired" like Dunlop, the famous tyre company. However, he was anything but lethargic. Born into a farming family of Scottish descent in the small city of Wangaratta in the north-east of Victoria, Australia in 1907, he began his medical career at 17 as an apprentice pharmacist before going to pharmacy college, and then, in 1930, he gained a scholarship to Melbourne University to study medicine.

Being from Victoria, the heartland of Australian Rules football, it was this game rather than rugby which he played in his youth and early years at college. His position was 'ruckman': one of the most important and physically demanding positions on the oval, it's the one who has to contest the centre bounces and stoppages. In rugby terms, it is probably most comparable to a lock, who plays a role in contesting line-outs. But in reality, as the ball in Aussie Rules restarts is almost always thrown straight up and high into the air rather than horizontally, the position is most similar to a centre in basketball.

The 6' 4", 14st 10lb Dunlop would only take up rugby in 1931, aged 24, when he joined the fourth team at Melbourne University Rugby Club. Once he finally started, he was clearly a natural and didn't waste any time, rapidly progressing through the grades into the first team. He was quickly selected for a Combined Universities team, then on to state representation for Victoria and, just a year after first picking up a rugby ball, he was called into the national team.

Dunlop said it was the thrill of running with the ball and the act of tackling, plus its international appeal, that made him prefer rugby to Aussie Rules. "Although I have been in rugby for so short a time, I like it better than my old game... The whole team gets into action at one time, and moves like one man in great dashes down the field, striving to defeat the opposing side and put the ball over the line... and tackling is more thrilling than anything in the Australian game."[175]

When selected to make his debut at No. 8 for Australia against the All Blacks at the Sydney Cricket Ground on 23 July 1932, he became the first Victoria-born player to represent the Wallabies. Dunlop couldn't, however, debut with a win as the visitors came out on top, 21-13.

"Functioning all the time as a team, smooth and polished as are all the sides New Zealand send us..." one of the local papers reported of the match.[176] Some things don't change too much in the world of rugby!

Victory might have eluded Dunlop that time, but there would be some sporting success in 1932 when he became his university's heavyweight boxing champion. Combining sport with his academic work, he was an industrious and hard-working student. But it wasn't all endeavour and graft; one obituary of him used the uniquely Australian word 'larrikin' to describe his college days, with one definition describing the term as meaning "a mischievous young person, an uncultivated, rowdy but good-hearted person", and another adding that it indicates "a person who acts with apparent disregard for social or political conventions".

Dunlop declined to play for Australia on their tour of South Africa and Rhodesia in 1933 due to his university commitments, but would pick up his second cap, as a lock, in a 25-11 win over New Zealand in August 1934. He flexed his hard-man credentials as he went into the match, with an only recently healed broken nose, sustained whilst boxing.

As the leader in the line-out and not being afraid to throw his weight around, he was a target for the New Zealand team. After just five minutes, one All Black pinned him at a ruck and another smashed into him. His nose was broken again. This didn't seem to faze Dunlop. Not only did he play on and complete the match in a famous victory, but according to a newspaper report, displayed "remarkable fortitude" and "played the game of his life, and was one of the outstanding forwards on the ground."[177]

After the game, with two beers acting as an anaesthetic, he then reset his own nose using a toothbrush up each nostril.

On graduating from university with first-class honours, he worked first as a house surgeon and registrar at the Royal Melbourne Hospital and then as registrar at the Royal Children's Hospital, Melbourne. In 1937 he sailed to London for further study at St Bart's Hospital and then worked as a specialist surgeon in the Emergency Medical Services at St Mary's Hospital, also in London.

St Mary's had a particularly good rugby team at that time, in a very competitive hospitals league, and Dunlop quickly established himself as a key member – for which he was rewarded with Barbarians selection (although a frozen Cardiff pitch stopped him ever getting to wear the famous black and white hoops). He also turned out for a Commonwealth XV whilst in London.

Then came the war.

Dunlop had been a reservist Captain in the Australian Army Medical Corps since 1935, and when hostilities were declared, he volunteered for the medical branch of the Australian Imperial Forces in London. He was posted first to Palestine, and then on being promoted to Major, served in campaigns in Greece and Crete. He worked there in casualty clearing stations and only narrowly avoided capture by the Germans, before being sent to North Africa, where he was the senior surgeon at the decisive Allied victory at Tobruk. This victory in Libya came at a huge cost, with approximately 6,000 Allied casualties. It was the Australian forces that suffered the most, with the Australian Official History of World War II stating they had 746 killed and 1,996 wounded.

Despite the exertions and dangers of war, Dunlop managed to keep up his rugby. He played for the Australian Army XV and, whilst in Palestine, also for a team in Jerusalem whose matches were held on a temporary pitch at the foot of the Mount of Olives.

His rugby playing would be severely curtailed but not fully stopped when the Japanese overran his hospital in Java in 1942. A fellow captured medic, Maurice Kinmonth, remembers the moment the hospital was formally handed over. A very short Japanese general arrived and Dunlop, with an already significant height advantage over his new captor, stood rigidly to attention. The general, by way of showing his displeasure at this perceived slight, drew his sword and flashed it repeatedly on either side of Dunlop's head. Dunlop didn't move or even blink, his eyes remaining fixed firmly forward until the general desisted and stormed off.

Dunlop, the staff and patients were marched off to a camp in Bandung, and although neither a combat soldier nor the most senior officer of the Allied forces contained there by the Japanese, he was by general consent made officer-in-charge. In January 1943 he was sent to Thailand, one of about 13,000 Australians among approximately 60,000 Allied POWs forced to work on the construction of the Burma Railway.

The most famous depiction of this part of World War II is the 1957 film, *The Bridge on the River Kwai*, and even that perhaps underplays the brutality the Japanese inflicted on their captives. The estimated number of civilian labourers and POWs who died during construction varies but the Australian Government figures suggest that of the 330,000 people who worked on the line, about 90,000 Asian labourers (mostly forcibly conscripted or lured by false promises of pay and unaware of their ultimate destination) and about 16,000 Allied prisoners died.

Conditions were abominable. Not only were the workers undernourished and dehydrated, but they were also denied medicine for diseases like dysentery, cholera and diarrhoea, which were rampant. Torture, humiliation and public executions were common. The construction of the Burma Railway is counted as a war crime.

Dunlop was made both the chief doctor and the commanding officer of more than 1,000 POWs in one section, known as 'Dunlop's Thousand'. This leadership, which he had only accepted reluctantly, made him responsible for choosing which men were healthy enough to work and then tending to the illnesses and injuries suffered after long hours of exhausting labour in the tropical heat.

Lacking even the most basic medical supplies, Dunlop and his fellow doctors managed to create an effective surgical hospital through a mix of ingenuity, improvisation and scavenging. Artificial legs hewn from bamboo and antiseptic saline delivered by a contraption built from bamboo, rubber tubing and sawn-off beer bottles were just two of their innovations.

While necessity is the mother of invention, Dunlop, during these dark days, could be described as its father, and countless POWs owed their lives to his ability to improvise surgical equipment.

Dunlop wrote about that spirit in the preface to the published versions of his war diaries. "Those in the medical services had the stimulus of the stark needs of a deluge of piteously ill men, and most doctors were fearless in approaches to our captors. However, much of the salvage of sick and broken men was achieved by securing the involvement of the whole stricken force in the sharing of slender resources, money and food, and contributing ingenious improvisations and gifts of labours of love out of their ebbing energy."[178]

Dunlop himself suffered terribly: amoebic dysentery, beriberi, tropical ulcers and malaria were some of what he endured. He was also subjected to severe beatings and threatened with execution.

"Part hero, part saint," said one of his colleagues, whilst another saw him as "a lighthouse of sanity in a universe of madness and suffering".[179]

Reading the accounts of his time on the railway, it is his immense stoicism and discipline even in the face of extreme provocation, particularly during the extra-difficult months when there was an intense pressure to complete their section of the railway, that shines through. That and his fierce commitment to keeping as many of his men as healthy as possible, despite the terrible obstacles they were facing.

But even during this horrendous period, he didn't forget about rugby.

In 1943, whilst in a POW camp, he led an Australian team in a fixture against a British XV. His opposing captain that day was Dr A W 'Bill' Frankland, known as the 'grandfather of the allergy' due to his groundbreaking research in this area. Bill noted in his autobiography that he was surprised but delighted to see that Dunlop had his St Mary's Hospital rugby shirt with him, which he proudly wore.[180] I assume the Japanese didn't allow many personal effects to be brought into the captivity, so it's a heart-warming thought that one of the few things Dunlop grabbed was his old club's jersey.

Once the railway was completed, he was moved first to a military hospital, and then a large hospital camp, where he was when the war came to an end. Demobilised in 1946, he returned home and to domestic medicine, married his fiancée – from whom he had been away for so many years – and started a family. Over the following years he received many honours, including a knighthood in 1969, was named Australian of the Year in 1977 and in 1988, on the occasion of Australia's bicentennial, he was included on a list of 200 people who had "made the country great". He also encouraged the training of Asian medical personnel in Australia, and in 1969 he returned to south-east Asia during the Vietnam War as the leader of the Australian surgical team caring for civilians.

His love of rugby remained, despite his many varied other interests, and though long retired, it still gave him an opportunity to show his legendary toughness even in old age. Wallaby hooker Tommy Lawton recalls a pre-match dinner before the 1989 British Lions Test in Brisbane.

"Finishing a speech to the team, Weary was walking back from the podium and after a misstep, fell flat on his face. Back on his feet, a quick look at Weary's nose smeared to one side told everyone present it was broken. 'Billy!' Weary barked to 22-cap lock William 'Billy' Campbell, who was studying to be a surgeon. 'Get me my toothbrush and a fork'. As the preparing team sat watching (and wincing), there were audible crunches as Campbell helped to straighten out Weary's mashed nose, with the patient demanding updates: 'Is it straight yet, Bill?

What about now, Bill? Is it straight?' He got fixed up, then came back to finish his dinner and drink."[181]

Dunlop died in Melbourne on 2 July 1993 and was wearing his beloved Wallabies jersey when he suffered a fatal collapse. He was given a state funeral with full military honours, which was attended by over 10,000 people. His remains were later cremated and floated down the River Kwai. There are three statues of him in Australia and a suburb of Canberra is named after him. The Weary Dunlop Shield has, since 2011, been contested by the NSW Waratahs and Melbourne Rebels and Dunlop was inducted into the Australian Rugby Union Hall of Fame in 2008, once again a first for a Victorian.

However good a rugby player Dunlop was – and more Australia caps would have followed if not for his medical career and then the war – it will always be his compassionate medical care and leadership during the dark days of World War II for which he will be best remembered.

Famous author Laurens van der Post, who was held captive alongside Dunlop, pays him this tribute: "I have the testimony of hundreds of Australians who had served with me and who accompanied Weary to Burma and Siam that he was both their inspiration and the main instrument of their physical and spiritual survival."[182]

And what of Bill Griffiths, the young aircraftman that Dunlop saved from a Japanese bayonet? Despite his terrible injuries and never recovering his sight, he survived three years in a POW camp and returned to Britain to work for St Dunstan's, a charity helping blind service personnel. He would marry and have a family, was awarded an MBE in 1977 and passed away aged 92 in 2012.

For Bill and the countless other men and women he saved, Ernest Edward 'Weary' Dunlop is truly the hardest player in this book.

AUTHOR ACKNOWLEDGEMENTS

A LARGE PORTION of this book was written during the Coronavirus pandemic, and so the opportunity to disappear into Edwardian Scotland, 1960s Newport, 1990s Canada or modern-day Namibia, among the other rugby worlds which I briefly inhabited, came as an enjoyable and timely distraction from the worries of 2020.

One of the many unwelcome results of the pandemic has been that the economic challenges facing newspapers and magazines have become significantly more acute: some have closed, others have cut their staff and few are prospering. But this book would have not been possible without the work of a host of journalists, spanning over 110 years. There are too many to name here, but a big thank you to each and every one of them. It's a far from perfect industry, but we'll miss it when it's gone. So, if you like reading a particular newspaper, magazine or website, please consider spending a few quid a month on keeping it going.

A huge thank you to all the team at Y Lolfa, for taking a chance on me with *Absolutely Huge*, and then trusting me again to take on the stewardship of this book. Our twenty hard men are very different to Gethin Hughes, although I have again been able to feature a Welsh player having a mishap with a bull! In particular I'd like to say a big thank you to Lefi Gruffudd for his continued confidence and advice. And to Carolyn Hodges, who despite her protestations is becoming quite the rugby expert, and shared all her editorial skills, positivity and wise suggestions to improve the text greatly. *Diolch i'r ddau!*

I would also like to thank Katie Field, who first reviewed the text and brought all her experience of writing about rugby to sharpen the first draft.

Thank you also to Tonino Anzante for using his expert translation skills to support some additions in the chapters on French players.

I also had the help of a number of the players featured, or their former teammates, in shaping the chapters. Their time, support and openness in talking to me is hugely appreciated. And I won't lie – as a rugby fan first and foremost, I did get a little jolt when I saw the likes of Bakkies Botha or Lee Byrne flash up on my phone. Thanks boys!

I would also like to give a shout-out to Matt Cutler, who, with our 'project' a decade ago, began the process that got me going with rugby writing. Cheers, mate!

A thank you to all the team at my day job as Editor of *Bio Market Insights* – Alex, Rosie, Liz, Ryan and Tom – for letting me write every day and learn more about telling stories from around the world.

A shout-out also to the 23rd Old Gorians – the cream of Swansea society and a constant source of entertainment, even if it has been mainly on WhatsApp in 2020 – here's to a few more trips to the pub in 2021!

A love of rugby, reading and writing comes from my parents, so the origins of this book are with John and Anne Upton in Swansea, and would not have grown without the love and support of my family in both Wales and London – Jamie, Lucy, Pablo, Marion, Elliot, Oscar, Daphne and Josephine.

A huge thank you also to my Irish family – Pat, Chris, Aoife, Caroline, Catherine, Paul, Henry, Éala and Méabh for their support. And for those reading this in Monahan's bar in Athlone – apologies for only selecting two Irishmen!

This book would not have been possible without the massive support of my wife Eimear. Our daughter Iseult was born during the writing of *Absolutely Huge* and our son Séamus arrived during this book's production, so time to do 'book stuff' was at a premium and without Eimear's assistance I never would have been able to do it. Your support means everything and I can't thank you enough.

Séamus himself is developing quite a fondness for chasing a ball around. If he gains a love of the game, I'd like to think being surrounded by rugby books, magazines, newspapers and a dad watching lots of clips on YouTube during his first year might have played a small part!

And finally, I'd like to thank all the players in this book. It's been a pleasure learning about them and their lives and careers. If some think I have been too critical, I apologise, but I've wanted to be honest: none of them are angels, but all are great players and it's this mix that has ultimately given them the reputations they have.

I hope you enjoy reading this book as much as I have enjoyed writing it.

Thank you for the support.

Luke Upton
London, September 2020

@MrLukeUpton
LukeUpton84@gmail.com
www.lukeupton.co.uk

BIBLIOGRAPHY

Publications

BARNES, David and BURNS, Peter with GRIFFITHS, John, *Behind the Thistle – Playing Rugby for Scotland* (Arena Sport, 2016)

BENNETT, Phil and THOMAS, Graham, *Phil Bennett – The Autobiography* (HarperCollins, 2004)

BRADFORD, Roy and DILLON, Martin, *Rogue Warrior of the SAS* (Arrow Books, 1989)

BRENNAN, Trevor with THORNLEY, Gerry, *Heart and Soul* (Red Rock Press, 2007)

BYRNE, Lee with MORGAN, Richard, *Lee Byrne – The Byrne Identity* (Y Lolfa, 2017)

CASTLETON, David, *In the Mind's Eye – The Blinded Veterans of St Dunstan's* (Pen & Sword Military, 2013)

DAVIDSON, Max, *Fields of Courage – The Bravest Chapters in Sport* (Little, Brown, 2011)

DAVIES, Lynn, *Hard Men of Welsh Rugby* (Y Lolfa, 2011)

DOOLEY, Wade with GREENBERG, Gerry, *The Tower and the Glory – The Wade Dooley Story* (Mainstream Publishing, 1992)

DUNLOP, E E, *The War Diaries of Weary Dunlop* (Penguin, 2010)

ENGLISH, Tom, *No Borders: Playing Rugby for Ireland – New 2018 Grand Slam Edition* (Birlinn, 2018)

GIBBS, Scott with LAWRENSON, David, *Getting Physical* (Ebury Press, 2000)

GRAY, Wynne, *Buck – The Wayne Shelford Story* (Moa, 1990)

GROWDEN, Greg, *Inside the Wallabies: The Real Story – The Players, the Politics and the Games from 1908 to Today* (Allen & Unwin, 2010)

JOHN, Barry, *Barry John's World of Rugby* (W H Allen, 1978)

JOHNSON, Martin, *Martin Johnson – The Autobiography* (Headline, 2003)

JOHNSON, Tony and MCCONNELL, Lynn, *Behind the Silver Fern – Playing Rugby for New Zealand* (Arena Sport, 2017)

JONES, Adam with HARRIES, Ross, *Bomb* (Mainstream Publishing, 2015)

JONES, Stephen, ENGLISH, Tom, CAIN, Nick and BARNES, David, *Behind the Lions – Playing rugby for the British & Irish Lions* (Arena Sport, 2013)

MCGEECHAN, Ian with JAMES, Steve, *The Lions – When the Going Gets Tough* (Hodder, 2017)

MCGEECHAN Ian and JONES Stephen, *Lion Man – The Autobiography* (Simon and Schuster, 2009)

MORRIS, Dai and WILLIAMS, Martyn, *Shadow – The Dai Morris Story* (Y Lolfa, 2012)

REYBURN, Ross, *John Dawes – The Man Who Changed the World of Rugby* (Y Lolfa, 2013)

SCALLY, John, *100 Irish Rugby Greats* (Mainstream Publishing, 2012)

SEWELL, E H D, *The Rugby Football Roll of Honour* (T C & E C Jack Ltd, 1919)

THOMAS, Clem, *The History of the British Lions* (Mainstream Publishing, 1996)

TOSSELL, David, *Nobody Beats Us – The Inside Story of the 1970s Wales Rugby Team* (Mainstream Publishing, 2009)

TURNER, Brian, *Meads* (Hodder Moa Beckett, 2002)

UMAGA, Tana & THOMAS, Paul, *Up Close – Tana Umaga* (Hodder Moa, 2007)

WINDSOR, Bobby and JACKSON, Peter, *The Iron Duke – The Life and Times of a Working-Class Rugby Hero* (Mainstream Publishing, 2010)

Periodicals

The Courier-Mail (Brisbane)
Daily Mail (UK)
The Daily Telegraph (UK)
The Drum (UK)

The Guardian (UK)
The Herald (Melbourne)
Hérault Tribune (France)
The Independent (UK)
The Irish Times
The London Gazette
Macleans magazine (Canada)
The Morning Bulletin (Queensland)
La Nacion (Argentina)
The New Zealand Herald
The Referee (Sydney)
Rugby Journal
The Rugby Paper
Rugby World
The Times (UK)
Western Mail (Wales)

Websites
All Blacks Official Site
Americas Rugby News
BBC News
BBC Sport (Rugby Union)
ESPN Rugby
Joe (Ireland)
Official Lions Rugby
RTE
Rugby Dump
Rugby News Service
Rugby Relics
Sky Sports
The Spinoff (New Zealand)
Sport24 (South Africa)
Stuff (New Zealand)
Ultimate Rugby
Wales Online

NOTES

1   Barry John, *Barry John's World of Rugby*

2   Stewart McClean, 'Blair 'Paddy' Mayne, The British Lions tour of South Africa 1938', Rugby Relics (World Rugby Museum), www.rugbyrelics.com/museum/biogs/Mayne-RB-I-1937.htm

3   Peter Crutchley, 'Blair Mayne: Lions legend 80 years ago and a decorated soldier', BBC Northern Ireland, 25 July 2018, www.bbc.co.uk/sport/rugby-union/44725686

4   John O'Sullivan, 'Paddy Mayne: The bravehearted Irish Lion who joined the SAS', *Irish Times*, 2 June, 2017, www.irishtimes.com/sport/rugby/international/paddy-mayne-the-bravehearted-irish-lion-who-joined-the-sas-1.3105452

5   Roy Bradford and Martin Dillon, *Rogue Warrior of the SAS*, p.14

6   Crutchley, 'Blair Mayne: Lions legend 80 years ago and a decorated soldier'

7   *The London Gazette*, 19 October 1943, www.thegazette.co.uk/London/issue/36217/supplement/4661

8   Bradford and Dillon, *Rogue Warrior of the SAS*, p.165

9   ibid., p.177

10   UK Parliament, 'Lt. Col Paddy Mayne, Early Day Motion #317', 14 June 2005, https://edm.parliament.uk/early-day-motion/28523/lt-col-paddy-mayne

11   Bradford and Dillon, *Rogue Warrior of the SAS*, p.230

12   Simon Hunter, 'Blair Mayne SAS Diary Released', BBC News, 23 September 2011, www.bbc.co.uk/news/uk-northern-ireland-15036691

13   Bradford and Dillon, *Rogue Warrior of the SAS*, p.15

14   Frank Keating, 'From the Vault: a new nadir for Welsh rugby', *The Guardian*, October 1991, republished 7 October 2008, www.theguardian.com/sport/blog/2008/oct/07/rugby.wales.samoa

15   Rob Wildman, 'Brian Lima in groove to break record', *The Daily Telegraph*, 24 August 2007, www.telegraph.co.uk/sport/rugbyunion/international/2319675/Brian-Lima-in-groove-to-break-record.html

16   James Mortimer, 'Henry still in awe of his injured captain', All Blacks, 2 November 2011, www.allblacks.com/news/henry-still-in-awe-of-his-injured-captain

[17] Max Davidson, *Fields of Courage – The Bravest Chapters in Sport*, p.64

[18] Pranav Soneji, 'Buck's All Black Fizz', BBC Sport, 24 October 2002, http://news.bbc.co.uk/sport1/hi/rugby_union/international/2354565.stm

[19] Wynne Gray, *Buck – The Wayne Shelford Story*, p.132

[20] 'France "loaded" on drugs for infamous 1986 All Blacks "Battle of Nantes" test', Stuff.co.nz, 25 February 2015, https://www.stuff.co.nz/sport/rugby/all-blacks/66622194/france-loaded-on-drugs-for-infamous-1986-all-blacks-battle-of-nantes-test

[21] 'France Drug Scandal No Surprise I knew they were on something', *Telegraph* and *AFP*, 25 February 2015, www.telegraph.co.uk/sport/rugbyunion/international/france/11433808/France-drug-scandal-no-surprise-I-knew-they-were-on-something-says-former-All-Black-Wayne-Buck-Shelford.html

[22] Graham Clutton, 'Semi Final Injustice Still Pains former Wales star Huw Richards', *The Daily Telegraph*, 14 October 2011, https://www.telegraph.co.uk/sport/rugbyunion/international/wales/8827699/Rugby-World-Cup-2011-semi-final-injustice-still-pains-former-Wales-star-Huw-Richards-the-villain-of-87.html

[23] Gray, *Buck*, p.140

[24] Mark Orders, 'The story of the brutal punch that knocked out a Wales player and saw the victim sent off', Wales Online, 19 May 2020, https://www.walesonline.co.uk/sport/rugby/rugby-news/story-brutal-punch-wales-famous-16419796

[25] Gray, *Buck*, p.126

[26] ibid., p.129

[27] Sam Tremlett, 'What Is The Haka?' *Rugby World*, 20 September 2019, https://www.rugbyworld.com/tournaments/rugby-world-cup-2019/what-is-the-haka-100373

[28] Max Boyce, 'The Pontypool Front Row', *We All Had Doctors' Papers* (1975, EMI), Track 11

[29] Bobby Windsor and Peter Jackson, *The Iron Duke – The Life and Times of a Working-Class Rugby Hero*, p.110

[30] ibid., p.68

[31] Stephen Jones, Tom English, Nick Cain and David Barnes, *Behind the Lions – Playing rugby for the British & Irish Lions*, p.186

[32] ibid., p.187

[33] Windsor and Jackson, *The Iron Duke*, p.85

[34] ibid., p.112

35   ibid., p.184

36   Justin Gregory, 'An oral history of the time Colin Meads played rugby with a broken arm', The Spinoff, 21 August 2017, https://thespinoff.co.nz/sports/21-08-2017/an-oral-history-of-the-time-colin-meads-played-rugby-with-a-broken-arm/

37   Brian Turner, Meads, p.58

38   ibid., p.27

39   ibid., p.48

40   ibid., p.53

41   Greg Growden, 'Ken Catchpole was Australian player most feared by All Blacks', ESPN Rugby, 22 December 2017, https://www.espn.co.uk/rugby/story/_/id/21842174/ken-catchpole-was-australian-player-most-feared-all-blacks

42   Greg Growden, Inside the Wallabies – The Real Story, the Players, the Politics and the Games from 1908 to Today, p.65

43   Turner, Meads, p.64

44   ibid., p.52

45   Dai Morris and Martyn Williams, Shadow – The Dai Morris Story, p.67

46   Ross Reyburn, John Dawes – The Man Who Changed the World of Rugby

47   Turner, Meads, p.52

48   Mark Reason, 'The Pinetree who gave New Zealand shelter, Sir Colin Meads', Stuff.co.nz, 22 August 2017, https://www.stuff.co.nz/sport/rugby/opinion/96021871/mark-reason--eulogy-to-a-sportsman-the-pinetree-who-gave-new-zealand-shelter

49   Steven Morris, 'All Blacks' Terminator springs a big surprise in Devon', The Guardian, 1 November 2007, https://www.theguardian.com/uk/2007/nov/01/rugbyunion.sport

50   ibid.

51   Tana Umaga & Paul Thomas, Up Close – Tana Umaga

52   'Charvis defends under-fire Umaga', BBC Sport, 4 November 2005, http://news.bbc.co.uk/sport1/hi/rugby_union/international/4404830.stm

53   Rob Houwing, 'Schalk: You knew Jerry was coming', Sport24, 18 June 2015, www.sport24.co.za/Rugby/Super15/Schalk-You-knew-Jerry-was-coming-20150618

54   Lee Byrne with Richard Morgan, Lee Byrne – The Byrne Identity, p.72

55   Deidre Mussen and Michael Forbes, 'Jerry Collins funeral: Tributes flow, legend tried to protect daughter in fatal crash' Stuff.co.nz, 17 June, 2015, https://www.stuff.co.nz/sport/rugby/all-blacks/69474272/jerry-collins-funeral-tributes-flow-legend-tried-to-protect-daughter-in-fatal-crash

56   ESPN Staff, 'Jonah Lomu: Jerry Collins died protecting his baby daughter', ESPN, 18 June 2015, http://en.espn.co.uk/newzealand/rugby/story/266919.html

57   Deidre Mussen and Michael Forbes, 'Jerry Collins funeral: Tributes flow, legend tried to protect daughter in fatal crash'

58   Joe Chidley, 'An Underground Hero', Macleans magazine, 28 November 1994, https://archive.macleans.ca/article/1994/11/28/An-Underground-Hero

59   'Canada vs New Zealand 1991 RWC Quarter-Final', YouTube https://www.youtube.com/watch?v=Xvi8FwndcFE

60   Tim Glover, 'Canadians have the travel bug: Tim Glover reports on a transatlantic challenge for the men from the tundra', The Independent, 15 October 1992

61   'Canada remembers great Hadley', Americas Rugby News, 29 March 2016, http://www.americasrugbynews.com/2016/03/29/canada-remembers-great-hadley/

62   E H D Sewell, The Rugby Football Roll of Honour

63   David Barnes and Peter Burns with John Griffiths, Behind the Thistle – Playing Rugby for Scotland, p.23

64   ibid., p.23

65   Clem Thomas, The History of the British Lions, p.50

66   David Walmsley, '1904: Bedell-Sivright pulls no punches', The Daily Telegraph, 30 June 2005, https://www.telegraph.co.uk/sport/rugbyunion/2361780/1904-Bedell-Sivright-pulls-no-punches.html

67   Sewell, The Rugby Football Roll of Honour

68   'Death of D.R. Bedell-Sivright', The Referee (Sydney), 15 September 1915, https://trove.nla.gov.au/newspaper/article/129353461

69   Sewell, The Rugby Football Roll of Honour

70   The University of Edinburgh RFC Scholarship, https://rugby.eusu.ed.ac.uk/bedell-sivright-scholarship-fund

71   'Lions look back at 1997', Lions Rugby, 8 May 2011, www.lionsrugby.com/2011/05/08/lions-look-back-at-97/

72   Scott Gibbs with David Lawrenson, Getting Physical, p.117

73   Jones, English, Cain and Barnes, Behind the Lions, p.201

74 'Lions in South Africa 1997 – Part Two', YouTube, https://www.
    youtube.com/watch?v=snCjO6aDX5U
75 Gibbs with Lawrenson, *Getting Physical*, p.118
76 ibid., p.114
77 ibid., p.25
78 Steve Bale and Dave Hadfield, 'Gibbs' flight to St Helens outrages
    Swansea: Welsh and British Isles union centre switches codes for
    five-year contract and derides his former sport's efforts to keep
    him', *The Independent*, 20 April 1994, https://www.independent.
    co.uk/sport/rugby-union-gibbs-flight-to-st-helens-outrages-
    swansea-welsh-and-british-isles-union-centre-switches-1371346.
    html
79 Gibbs with Lawrenson, *Getting Physical*, p.60
80 Ian McGeechan and Stephen Jones, *Lion Man – The Autobiography*,
    p.252
81 Jones, English, Cain and Barnes, *Behind the Lions*, p.203
82 Gibbs with Lawrenson, *Getting Physical*, p.156
83 Tanya Aldred, 'Gibbs hangs up his boots at 33', *The Guardian*, 23
    January 2004, https://www.theguardian.com/sport/2004/jan/23/
    rugbyunion
84 Gavin Mortimer, 'The Master of Menace: French enforcer Gerard
    Cholley', *Rugby World*, 24 February 2016, www.rugbyworld.com/
    countries/france-countries/the-master-of-menace-french-enforcer-
    gerard-cholley-54416
85 Brendan Gallagher, 'England v France: Fran Cotton remembers
    classic encounters with the "scary hombres" of Les Bleus', *The Daily
    Telegraph*, 22 February 2013, https://www.telegraph.co.uk/sport/
    rugbyunion/international/england/9888721/England-v-France-Fran-
    Cotton-remembers-classic-encounters-with-the-scary-hombres-of-
    Les-Blues.html
86 David Tossell, *Nobody Beats Us – The Inside Story of the 1970s Wales
    Rugby Team*, p.217
87 ibid., p.217
88 '*Actions légendaires, Gérard Cholley met KO deux écossais*', Daily
    Motion, https://www.dailymotion.com/video/x3vdr97
89 Barnes, Burns and Griffiths, *Behind the Thistle*, p.274.
90 Tom English, 'Six Nations 2016: Milne brothers recall French
    battles', BBC Sport, 11 March 2016, https://www.bbc.co.uk/sport/
    rugby-union/35788754

91   Tony Johnson, Lynn McConnell, *Behind the Silver Fern – Playing Rugby for New Zealand*, p.204

92   Windsor and Jackson, *The Iron Duke*, p.224

93   'Trevor Brennan Misconduct Decision', European Professional Club Rugby, 16 March 2007, www.epcrugby.com/2007/03/16/trevor-brennan-misconduct-decision/

94   Trevor Brennan with Gerry Thornley, *Heart and Soul*, p.52

95   ibid., p.60

96   John Scally, *100 Irish Rugby Greats*

97   Brennan with Thornley, *Heart and Soul*, p.105

98   ibid., p.118

99   ibid., p.157

100 ibid., p.237

101 'Brennan blames fans for clash', RTE, 17 January 2007, www.rte.ie/sport/rugby/2007/0123/213671-brennan1/

102 'Brennan faces ban after "assault"', BBC Sport, 23 January 2007, http://news.bbc.co.uk/sport2/hi/rugby_union/my_club/ulster/6286055.stm

103 'Ulster fan wins six figure payout', BBC News Northern Ireland, 10 January 2008, http://news.bbc.co.uk/1/hi/northern_ireland/7181696.stm

104 Brennan with Thornley, *Heart and Soul*, p.258

105 ibid., p.164

106 Wade Dooley with Gerry Greenberg, *The Tower and the Glory – The Wade Dooley Story*, p.44

107 '1987 Five Nations Championship: Wales vs England – The Battle of Cardiff', YouTube https://www.youtube.com/watch?v=6ukm_T_nXqg&t=11s

108 Nelli Bird, 'Wales v England: 30 years since the 'Battle of Cardiff'', BBC Wales News, 10 February 2017, www.bbc.co.uk/news/uk-wales-38921762

109 Dooley with Greenberg, *The Tower and the Glory*, p.78

110 ibid., p.83

111 Jones, English, Cain and Barnes, *Behind the Lions*, p.279

112 Dooley with Greenberg, *The Tower and the Glory*, p.25

113 ibid., p.21

114 Jones, English, Cain and Barnes, *Behind the Lions*, p.298

115 Chris Foy, 'Wade Dooley's iron fist set to add some punch to RFU

police', *Daily Mail*, 22 December 2008, www.dailymail.co.uk/sport/
rugbyunion/article-1100494/Wade-Dooleys-iron-fist-set-add-punch-
RFU-police.html

[116] Barrie Fairhall, 'Dooley pulls no punches', *The Independent*, 8
October 1992, https://www.independent.co.uk/sport/rugby-union-
dooley-pulls-no-punches-1556220.html

[117] 'Springboks fined over "Justice for Bakkies" armband protest', *The
Guardian*, 25 October 2009, www.theguardian.com/sport/2009/
aug/25/south-africa-bakkies-botha-protest

[118] 'Smit worried by Botha precedent', BBC Sport, 3 July 2009, http://
news.bbc.co.uk/sport1/hi/rugby_union/8126583.stm

[119] Adam Jones with Ross Harries, *Bomb*, p.228

[120] ibid., p.331

[121] Craig Rodney, 'Jones calls Springbok actions "disgraceful"'as
pair are banned', *The Independent*, 4 August 2003, https://www.
independent.co.uk/sport/rugby/rugby-union/jones-calls-springbok-
actions-disgraceful-as-pair-are-banned-98915.html

[122] Michael Brown, 'Rugby: Butt latest in long list of thug attacks',
Herald on Sunday, 11 July 2010, https://www.nzherald.co.nz/sport/
news/article.cfm?c_id=4&objectid=10658036

[123] Craig Rodney, 'Jones calls Springbok actions "disgraceful" as pair
are banned'

[124] Phil Harlow, 'England line up for toughest test', BBC Sport, 20
November 2008, http://news.bbc.co.uk/sport1/hi/rugby_union/
english/7738076.stm

[125] 'Henry not surprised at Botha's nine-week ban', *The New Zealand
Herald*, 11 July, 2010, www.nzherald.co.nz/rugby/news/article.
cfm?c_id=351&objectid=10658073

[126] 'Smit unhappy at "silly" Botha', Sport24, 10 July 2010, https://
www.sport24.co.za/rugby/trinations/smit-unhappy-at-silly-botha-
20100710?cpid=2

[127] 'Bakkies Botha suspended for nine weeks after headbutt on Jimmy
Cowan', Rugby Dump, 10 July 2020, https://www.rugbydump.com/
news/bakkies-botha-suspended-for-nine-weeks-after-headbutt-on-
jimmy-cowan/

[128] 'Springboks enforcer Bakkies Botha admits "I was born to hurt
others"', Stuff.co.nz, 22 April 2020, https://www.stuff.co.nz/sport/
rugby/international/121173864/springboks-enforcer-bakkies-botha-
admits-i-was-born-to-hurt-others

129 'Bakkies Botha injures Marcos Ayerza with big charge towards tryline', Rugby Dump, 11 April 2013, https://rugbydump. com/news/ bakkies-botha-injures-marcos-ayerza-with-big-charge-towards-tryline/

130 'Disciplinary update: Tomás Lavanini (Argentina)', World Rugby, 7 October 2019, https://www.world.rugby/news/504346?lang=en

131 Jorge Búsico, 'Guido Petti y Tomás Lavanini, dos chicos que juegan como grandes', La Nacion, 24 October 2015, https://www.lanacion. com.ar/deportes/rugby/guido-petti-y-tomas-lavanini-dos-chicos-que-juegan-como-grandes-nid1839441

132 Jorge Búsico, 'Lavanini, la suspensión y el tiempo de su lado para madurar y crecer', La Nacion, 29 February 2016, https://www. lanacion.com.ar/deportes/rugby/lavanini-la-suspension-y-el-tiempo-de-su-lado-para-madurar-y-crecer-nid1875475

133 'Tomas Lavanini signs for Leicester Tigers', Ultimate Rugby, 6 May 2019, https://www.ultimaterugby.com/news/tomas-lavanini-signs-for-leicester-tigers/616260

134 David Ashdown, 'Jacques Burger: the new toughest guy in rugby?' The Independent, 25 September 2010, https://www.independent. co.uk/sport/rugby/rugby-union/news-comment/jacques-burger-the-new-toughest-guy-in-rugby-2089033.html

135 Nik Simon, 'Namibia captain Jacques Burger chasing World Cup win for last time as 60 injuries in two years will force his retirement', Daily Mail, 24 September 2015, https://www.dailymail. co.uk/sport/rugbyunion/article-3246909/Namibia-captain-Jacques-Burger-chasing-World-Cup-win-time-60-injuries-two-years-force-retirement.html

136 'My Life in Rugby: Former Saracens and Namibia flanker Jacques Burger', The Rugby Paper, 22 November 2019, https://www. therugbypaper.co.uk/featured-post/34291/my-life-in-rugby-former-saracens-and-namibia-flanker-jacques-burger/

137 ibid.

138 'Top five players of RWC 2011', Rugby News Service, Monday 24 October 2011, https://web.archive.org/web/20141112163158/http:// www.rugbyworldcup.com/home/news/newsid%3D2060306.html

139 Chris Hewett, 'Jacques Burger interview: Battle back to fitness', The Independent, 20 September 2013, https://www.independent.co.uk/ sport/rugby/rugby-union/news-comment/jacques-burger-interview-battle-back-to-fitness-8830503.html

140 Sean Ingle, 'Jacques Burger: You need the mentality that you want to hit somebody', *The Guardian*, 23 September 2015, https://www.theguardian.com/sport/2015/sep/23/jacques-burger-namibia-rugby-world-cup-new-zealand

141 Mick Cleary, 'Jacques Burger the bloodied hero of Saracens' rampage past Clermont into the Heineken Cup final', *The Daily Telegraph*, 27 April 2014, https://www.telegraph.co.uk/sport/rugbyunion/european-rugby/10791473/Jacques-Burger-the-bloodied-hero-of-Saracens-rampage-past-Clermont-into-the-Heineken-Cup-final.html

142 Sean Ingle, 'Jacques Burger: You need the mentality that you want to hit somebody'

143 Windsor and Jackson, *The Iron Duke*, p.112

144 Tom English, *No Borders: Playing Rugby for Ireland – New 2018 Grand Slam Edition*

145 Barnes, Burns and Griffiths, *Behind the Thistle*

146 'Armand Vaquerin, Une légende biterroise', *Hérault Tribune*, 28 September 2018, https://www.herault-tribune.com/articles/171936/rugby-armand-vaquerin-une-legende-biterroise

147 ibid.

148 Martin Johnson, *Martin Johnson – The Autobiography*, p.303

149 McGeechan and Jones, *Lion Man*, p.235

150 Johnson, *Martin Johnson – The Autobiography*, p.270

151 Chris Hewett, 'All Blacks Appeased by Ban', *The Independent*, 24 November 1997, https://www.independent.co.uk/sport/rugby-union-all-blacks-appeased-by-ban-1295940.html

152 Johnson, *Martin Johnson – The Autobiography*, p.313

153 ibid., p.313

154 ibid., p.304

155 Robert Kitson, Mike Averis and Simon Burnton, 'Fierce and menacing but not a thug', *The Guardian*, 18 October 2003, https://www.theguardian.com/sport/2003/oct/18/rugbyunion.rugbyworldcup2003

156 ibid.

157 ibid.

158 Ian McGeechan with Steve James, *The Lions – When the Going Gets Tough*, p.228

159 Mark Orders, 'The true story of the day Welsh rugby's hardest men were injured fighting a bull', Wales Online, 27 June 2020, https://

www.walesonline.co.uk/sport/rugby/rugby-news/true-story-day-welsh-rugbys-18493397

160 'Scotland 0 – Wales 6, The Kicking Game', ESPN (report from 2 February 1963), https://www.espn.co.uk/rugby/report?gameId=2012 0&league=180659

161 Lynn Davies, *Hard Men of Welsh Rugby*, p.100

162 Phil Bennett and Graham Thomas, *Phil Bennett – The Autobiography*

163 Alex Mead, 'Neath RFC', *Rugby Journal*, 23 September 2019, https:// www.therugbyjournal.com/rugby-blog/neath-rfc

164 Mark Orders, 'The brutal story of the most violent Welsh rugby match of the 1990s that was played 25 years ago', Wales Online, 19 November 2019, https://www.walesonline.co.uk/sport/rugby/rugby-news/welsh-rugby-neath-fight-1990s-15356192

165 *Sky Sports* Twitter video, 5 April 2019, https://twitter.com/ SkySportsRugby/status/1114102616735277056?ref_src=twsrc %5Etfw%7Ctwcamp%5Etweetembed%7Ctwterm%5E111410 2616735277056&ref_url=https%3A%2F%2Fwww.rugbyworld. com%2Fnews%2Fsebastien-chabal-performs-hong-kong-sevens-dressed-caveman-99152

166 Charlotte McEleny, 'Marriott Hotels dresses Sébastien Chabal as a French maid for comedic Hong Kong Sevens spot', *The Drum*, 6 April 2018, https://www.thedrum.com/news/2018/04/06/marriott-hotels-dresses-s-bastien-chabal-french-maid-comedic-hong-kong-sevens-spot

167 Paul Newman, 'Sébastien Chabal: Sea Bass swims with the Sharks', *The Independent*, 7 January 2006, https://www.independent.co.uk/ sport/rugby/rugby-union/s-bastien-chabal-sea-bass-swims-with-the-sharks-337056.html

168 Jennifer Howze and Corrine Abrams, 'Sebastien Chabal, the he-man who makes Frenchwomen swoon', *The Times*, 12 October 2007, https://www.thetimes.co.uk/article/sebastien-chabal-the-he-man-who-makes-frenchwomen-swoon-hprnkkmp6jx

169 Bryn Palmer, 'The Caveman Cometh, Rugby World Cup Blog', BBC Sport, 20 September 2007, https://www.bbc.co.uk/blogs/ rugbyworldcup/2007/09/the_caveman_cometh.html

170 Stephen Jones, 'Chabal: The Rasputin of rugby', *The Sunday Times*, 29 October 2017, https://www.thetimes.co.uk/article/chabal-the-rasputin-of-rugby-sbxrbjsgb

[171] 'Peace and love. I just don't like c***s', ESPN, 26 December 2014 http://en.espn.co.uk/scrum/rugby/story/251073.html

[172] Sarah Mockford, 'Rise and fall of Sebastien "Caveman" Chabal', *Rugby World*, 29 August 2012, https://www.rugbyworld.com/countries/france-countries/rise-and-fall-of-sebastien-caveman-chabal-22815

[173] Conor Heneghan, 'Available on a free: Overrated French forward with bushy beard and flowing locks', Joe.ie, February 2012, https://www.joe.ie/uncategorized/available-on-a-free-overrated-french-forward-with-bushy-beard-and-flowing-locks-31965

[174] David Castleton, *In the Mind's Eye – The Blinded Veterans of St Dunstan's*

[175] 'Victorian in Rugby Test', *The Herald* (Melbourne), 20 July 1932, https://trove.nla.gov.au/newspaper/article/242980325

[176] 'All Blacks Win, Ashes go to New Zealand', *Morning Bulletin* (Rockhampton, Queensland), 25 July 1932, https://trove.nla.gov.au/newspaper/article/55498593

[177] 'Played with Broken Nose', *The Courier-Mail* (Brisbane), 14 August 1934, https://trove.nla.gov.au/newspaper/article/36733059

[178] E E Dunlop, *The War Diaries of Weary Dunlop*, p.8

[179] Royal College of Surgeons, 'Plarr's Lives of the Fellows: Dunlop, Sir Ernest Edward' (1907–1993), https://livesonline.rcseng.ac.uk/client/en_GB/lives/search/detailnonmodal/ent:$002f$002fSD_ASSET$002f0$002fSD_ASSET:380102/one?qu=%22rcs%3A+E0079 19%22&rt=false%7C%7C%7CIDENTIFIER%7C%7C%7CResource+Identifier

[180] Paul Watkins, 'Obituary: Dr A W 'Bill' Frankland MBE, DM, FRCP', Imperial College London, 6 April 2020, https://www.imperial.ac.uk/news/196715/obituary-dr-bill-frankland-mbe-dm/

[181] Thomas Van Leuween, 'Weary Dunlop: A toothbrush, a fork, and a whole lot of fighting spirit', https://tlvanleeuwen.wordpress.com/weary-dunlop/

[182] Dunlop, *The War Diaries of Weary Dunlop*

By the same author:

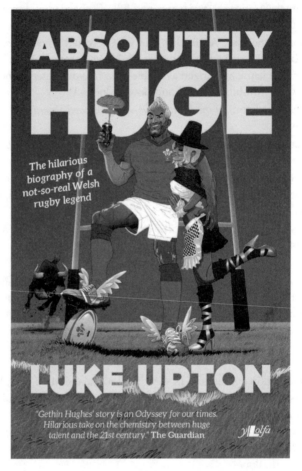

£9.99

Riotous spoof of the typical sports biography –
an affectionate send-up of modern rugby
and all the media hype that surrounds it.